ENERGIZING WORKPLACE PERFORMANCE

THE POWER OF PERFORMANCE MANAGEMENT

HAROLD S. RESNICK

ISBN: 978-1-4303-1275-8

For further information contact WSA at:
P. O. Box 3557
Ponte Vedra Beach, FL 32004-3557
Phone: 904/273-2558
Fax: 904/273-8213
Website: www.worksystems.com

Order online at:
www.lulu.com/content/812893

This book is dedicated to two women who have made

an extraordinary difference in my life.

The first is my mother, Ruth Resnick Siegel.
At age 98, this independent, energetic woman is the loving

matriarch of our family. She exemplifies a meaningful life,

providing service to others, and sharing her goodness and

wisdom with others each day.

The second is my wife, Barbara, who has taught me how to

live with meaning and love. Throughout the trials of life,

Barbara has given me the joy, honesty and purpose that can

only come from finding a true life partner.

Preface

A proven methodology to energize and convert human potential into extraordinary workplace performance.

If people are an organization's most important asset, why do so few organizations actually implement programs that help individuals achieve their potential? Research repeatedly shows that employees lack clarity regarding their roles, are unclear about their goals and success measures, do not feel they receive helpful feedback, do not receive adequate coaching, are not recognized for their accomplishments, and are frustrated by compensation systems that do not significantly differentiate between top performers and marginal ones.

Research also reveals that organizations that do implement performance management in a consistent, integrated manner achieve up to 34% productivity gains. Their work force is more strongly motivated which translates into increased customer satisfaction. There is also less turnover.

Energizing Workplace Performance provides the integrated systemic solution for maximizing employee potential and performance. The book is divided into three sections. The first section provides the rationale and research evidence for performance management, linking it directly to productivity, profitability and customer satisfaction.

The second section presents the framework for this comprehensive system. The last section provides the specific step-by-step methodology, enriched with real-life examples, that can transform individuals, groups and organizations.

In a time when competitive pressures reflect a global perspective, this book provides a beacon of light that shows how significant competitive advantage can be achieved simply by releasing and nurturing the potential and desire to achieve that resides in all of us.

Table of Contents

Introduction

I spent the first fifteen years of my career in the public sector as a teacher, a university professor, a senior administrator in a regional public school district, and then again as a professor. Throughout this period, I was continually frustrated by the dissension that seemed to exist so consistently between professional staff and their administration. I was dismayed that customers (students) were rarely the focus of whatever issue was at hand, and personal agendas prevailed. Politics, infighting and power drove organizational behavior. To be sure, I met and worked with many wonderful and gifted teachers. I had the privilege of partnering with many individuals who cared deeply about students and the learning process. Yet the dominant behavior throughout these various educational institutions did not emulate this same commitment to professionalism, performance or students.

During the latter years of my second professorship, I began to consult in the private sector. My professorship was at Boston University, and these were the heyday years of high technology along the famous Route 128 belt – well before Silicon Valley.

Because of the intense competition for talent in the high tech environment – especially for software engineers - the work I was asked to do by my clients was in the area of career development. I created and implemented a program that successfully reduced a 15% annual turnover rate for software engineers down to just over 5% within two years, for a major Division of a Fortune 100 company.

Based on that experience, the President of the company shared another concern with me. He said: "Our managers are like cheap wine. They all get promoted before their time. Virtually every one of my managers is doing his or her job for the very first time." He then asked if I thought I could develop a program that would give these very technically smart, but inexperienced managers the skills they needed to be successful in the job of managing people. We subsequently developed a management development program that was so successful it was adopted as the standard throughout that Fortune 100 Corporation.

Several years later, this same company acquired a young software company on the West Coast and needed to integrate their East Coast data processing organization with this new West Coast word processing business. This was a difficult technical challenge at that stage of the evolution of the information technology industry. Concurrently, they also needed to integrate more than 5000 people in 147 locations around the world, in the areas of field sales, field service, marketing and customer training.

As the consultant helping to design this integration, I recall saying at the end of a particularly exhausting, but exhilarating day, "This is so exciting I could spend my full energies working on it."

I arrived the next morning to find a job offer placed in my hand, and thus began my corporate career. Over the next several years, we successfully integrated these two companies - people, technologies, physical locations, and the business model for sales, service, marketing, manufacturing, customer training and customer support.

I was particularly struck by some of the differences I discovered in the corporate environment compared to my prior experiences in the public sector. First, everyone understood the mission. There was lots of discussion – even debates – along the way, but in the end, decisions were made by senior management and everyone followed their marching orders. Second, there was real effort placed in ensuring that everyone's individual goals were clearly understood and aligned with the goals of the organization. Third, once roles and goals were clear, people worked together to help each other achieve mutual success. Everyone was driven by the commonly understood mission.

The scorecard was clear. Revenue, market share, technology leadership, customer satisfaction, profitability and shareholder value drove our behavior. Although measures were not always aligned and could occasionally be in conflict, they were the guideposts for success. The largest difference between this environment and my public sector career wasn't the workload or the reward system. It was the agreement on organizational goals and the subsequent development of an aligned workforce to achieve those goals.

Unfortunately, organizational alignment is not a guaranteed thing – and certainly not permanent. It requires ongoing reinforcement and continuous course corrections. An old Chinese proverb states, "Success is the last rung of the ladder to failure." Another similar homily is, "Success sows the seeds of its own destruction."

In organizational life, success often leads to complacency. Complacency leads to arrogance. Arrogance leads to denial of truths and resistance to change. The result is the "internally focused organization." But the external world changes, often leading to the internal misalignment that causes so many once-great companies to fall from their lofty heights.

A common sense of purpose, alignment to that purpose, clarity of individual roles and responsibilities and aligned support systems require ongoing diligence. Beware the competitor who has achieved this alignment. He is indeed dangerous, for his people can achieve miracles.

In 1984, I activated my long-felt entrepreneurial desire to start my own company and see if I could bring what I had learned from others to my own business. I founded Work Systems Associates, Inc. (WSA), determined to see whether I could make an independent living as an organizational development consultant. Over the next fifteen years, WSA grew to become a multi-million dollar consulting firm serving clients throughout North and South America, Europe and the Middle East. Our industry focus was threefold: high technology, large-scale engineering-construction projects, and technical manufacturing environments.

During these years, the consulting team at WSA developed products and services in a variety of areas, including management and leadership development, live project team alignment, continuous improvement (TQM), strategic planning, executive development, systemic organizational change, and performance management systems.

An examination of all these services reveals a common thread: aligning the organization and its workforce, and then developing the competence of both the organization and its employees to achieve their established goals.

In the mid-nineties, I founded another company called Generation21 Learning Systems, LLC (Gen21). Gen21 was one of the very first web-based training and knowledge management systems. We invented the use of "learning objects" as the basis for creating asynchronous training programs that could provide customized training programs "on the fly" in response to student's test scores.

Gen21 was headquartered in Boston, with its Technology Center in Golden, Colorado. Once again, I discovered the same principles regarding organizational and workforce alignment. I traveled to Denver once every month to ensure alignment regarding our direction and projects for the next month. Somehow, ideas started to drift apart within days of each monthly meeting as a consequence of new customer requests, new technology ideas, sales opportunities, etc. The next month we had to review, re-align and often undo some of the work of the previous month. Fortunately, the good results outweighed the misalignments and the company was successfully acquired by Renaissance Learning (Nasdaq: RLRN) in 1999.

Having sold Generation21 and completed the transfer of the existing WSA clients to the other Boston-based clients, my wife, Barbara, and I moved to Ponte Vedra Beach, Florida in 1999.

Since that time, I have continued to work with many companies and have provided leadership development programs for another several thousand individuals. Throughout these experiences, I have seen the same issue time and time again: well intended, skilled individuals frustrated in their attempt to provide their employers with the level of contribution and value they know they have the potential to provide.

The pervasiveness of this issue comes down to a few fundamental truths. First, successful organizations must have a compelling vision, a mission, and a strategic plan or path forward to achieve their vision. Second, people require a sense of purpose and meaningfulness in their work and in their lives or they remain unfulfilled, and thus contribute far less than their potential. Third, if we can align the vision of the organization to the need for meaningfulness that people seek in their lives and then provide clear expectations and success measures, the results are extraordinary…even unstoppable.

But somehow, this is harder to do than it is to describe. And that is the essence and purpose of this book. Over a lifetime of working with hundreds of organizations and tens of thousands of individuals, I have developed a unique approach to creating this alignment through a system that is commonly called performance management. My intention and hope is that the contents of this book will provide all those who read it with an understanding of why and how this system works, so they can apply it for themselves and their organizations.

Thank you for the opportunity to present this information to you. I hope you enjoy reading it as much as I have enjoyed writing it.

H.S.R.

PART I

The Case for
Performance Management

CHAPTER 1

The Realities of the Workplace

Think about the ideal place to work.

It's an environment in which employees and the organization are fully aligned and committed to a common vision or purpose. There is an excitement – an enthusiasm – a shared sense of mission or purpose – and a collective drive to succeed together. Employees feel responsible, accountable for their performance, and empowered to act on behalf of customers and their organizations. There is a sense of a real team spirit, and people help each other toward their common purpose. Everyone knows exactly what is needed and their role in helping to achieve it. It is intense, focused, and driven. And…in the midst of all this intense, purposeful activity with a drive toward success…people are having fun. They enjoy their work. They enjoy working with each other. They enjoy serving their customers. They celebrate their successes together and rapidly analyze and take corrective action when actions do not achieve the desired results. The focus is on solving problems, not blaming others.

Can workplaces like this be found? Absolutely! They are often found in smaller, younger, entrepreneurial environments. They are found where the owner is also the leader. The focus is on creating success for everyone – first for customers, then for the employees, then for the enterprise. Everyone is part of the action.

This environment is not limited to young entrepreneurial organizations. It can be found in organizations of all sizes and shapes, all ages, private, public and non-profit. It is most commonly found in the early days of an enterprise.

Why is this so? Over time, successful organizations grow and it is this success that plants the seeds that potentially create frustration in the workplace. Growth creates the need for more people, more products, more services, and more customers – a good thing. But it also creates increased complexity, which often results in less focus, more diversity of activity, and bureaucracy. As organizations mature, they must continue to apply the tools that maintain this focus and enthusiasm relentlessly or they will surely drift toward mediocrity.

Consider the following statements by managers in many organizations. Ask yourself whether you have heard (or even said) statements similar to these yourself.

- I know that I should be sitting down with my employees to set their goals and performance measures. But we don't have the time for those kinds of meetings. We're under pressure to get the business done and I just can't take the time for that kind of soft stuff.

- I can tell people what to do, but some of the things I really care about are just too hard to measure. Take teamwork, for example. How do you measure that objectively? Since I can't be sure that all my measures would be absolutely objective, I'm better off not trying – saves me a lot of time and I won't get into trouble with Human Resources.

- I know I should be giving my employees feedback about the areas where I'm not happy with their performance. But I'm afraid of how they might react, and the result could be even more disgruntled and de-motivated employees. So I'll take what I can get and hope that they'll "get it" over time (which of course doesn't happen).

- I have several people who have the same job title and job description. Some are better than others, but it wouldn't be fair to give them different goals. After all, they have the same job so I guess I'm stuck with the "lowest common denominator."

- Our work environment is just too volatile for me to set goals with people. The situation changes weekly – even daily – and no goals would stay in place long enough for them to work.

- I don't see the point of worrying too much about this stuff. Our compensation system is so restrictive that I have almost no room to pay people differently anyway. And if I can't make real differences in their pay, it's not fair for me to set significantly different expectations or demands from them.

The situation is no better when examined from the employee's perspective. Look around in your own work environment. It's likely you can find all of the following:

- Employees who are unhappy, disgruntled, and perhaps even hostile to their own organization. They show up, do the minimum work required and take every opportunity to complain about their own organization, their supervisor, their co-workers, etc. Everyone but themselves. They do just enough to maintain their position and function in the company and become the "walking wounded."

- Employees who consistently underperform below their capabilities and below expectations set for them. Yet no one seems willing to address it or do anything about it. So their underperformance is tolerated, which causes both extra work and resentment among their co-workers.

- Employees who want to do well, but are genuinely frustrated by the limitations and restrictions of their work environment. They may not have the resources to do their work. They may not feel authorized or empowered to act. They may not have the information they need. Whatever the reason, their own frustration (often quite legitimate) causes individual underperformance and reduced organizational effectiveness and productivity.

- Well-intended employees who are working hard to do the right thing, but don't know how to do it, or even what the right thing to do is. So they put forward lots of effort that goes for naught or even needs to be undone or redone.

- Organizational re-work that is simply accepted as part of the way it is – often cased by insufficient time to do it properly. Said differently, employees that never have enough time to do it right, but always have enough time to do it over.

- Employees who are simply not trained in how to do their jobs. It is assumed that they will "catch it" over time – but the lack of training or well-defined work processes or methods causes ongoing errors and diminished productivity.

Harris Poll Research

In his recent book, The Eighth Habit[1]," Stephen Covey describes research conducted by Harris Interactive (the originators of the Harris Poll). In the 2004 timeframe, Harris Interactive surveyed 23,000 U.S. residents employed full-time within key industries and in key functional areas. The outcome of their research is both compelling and alarming. The results are highlighted below:

- Only 37% said they have a clear understanding of what their organization is trying to achieve and why.
- Only 1 in 5 was enthusiastic about their team's and organization's goals.
- Only 1 in 5 said they have a clear line of sight between their tasks and their team's and organization's goals.
- Only half were satisfied with the work they accomplished each week.
- Only 15% felt that their organization fully enables them to execute key goals.
- Only 15% felt they worked in a high-trust environment.
- Only 17% felt their organization fosters open communication that is respectful of differing opinions and that results in new and better ideas.
- Only 10% felt their organization holds people accountable for results.
- Only 20% fully trusted the organization they work for.
- Only 13% have high trust, highly cooperative working relationships with other groups or departments.[2]

1. Covey, Stephen R. The Eighth Habit. New York: Free Press, 2004. Pp. 2-3.
2. Harris Interactive.com. The Harris Poll #38 *"Many U.S. Employees Have Negative Attitudes To Their Jobs, Employers, and Top Managers,"* May 6, 2005.

And these are the results from the United States – arguably the most productive country in the history of the world!

Is this the best we can do? Are our organizations destined to be frustrating, underperforming entities? Are our individuals destined to have their spirits crushed and their desires to achieve and grow thwarted at every turn?

Not at all! In the midst of these findings, there are people and organizations who are excited, productive, empowered, performing and achieving results at levels that far exceed their competitors. There are many factors that create these results. Performance management is among the most powerful interventions.

Gallup Research

In 1997, the Gallup Organization set out to determine what a strong, vibrant workplace looks like.[3] Clearly, it begins with the satisfaction of its employees. Which organizations attract the most talented employees, and which organizations are able to keep them? Why is this so?

The results of this research were published in 1999 in a book entitled: First, Break All the Rules, written by Marcus Buckingham and Curt Coffman.[4] Over the course of twenty-five years, the Gallup Organization interviewed over a million employees, asking them hundreds of different questions on every conceivable aspect of the workplace. Then they sifted through the data piece by piece to find the most consistent, validated core elements of a work environment that attracts and retains the best and most talented employees.

They discovered that measuring the strength of a workplace in attracting, retaining and motivating its employees can be simplified to twelve questions. If an employee can answer these twelve questions in the positive, the strength of the work environment is manifested in low voluntary turnover, high motivation, and high employee productivity.

3. The Gallup Organization. *"The Employee Side of the HumanSigma Equation."* The Q12 research and programs. www.gallupconsulting.com. Updated annually, 2007.
4. Buckingham, Marcus and Coffman, Curt. *First, Break All The Rules*. New York: Simon and Schuster, 1999.

These questions are:

1. Do I know what is expected of me at work?
2. Do I have the materials and equipment I need to do my work right?
3. At work, do I have the opportunity to do what I do best every day?
4. In the last seven days, have I received recognition for doing good work?
5. Does my supervisor, or someone at work, care about me as a person?
6. Is there someone at work who encourages my development?
7. At work, do my opinions seem to count?
8. Does the mission of my company make me feel my job is important?
9. Are my co-workers committed to doing quality work?
10. Do I have a best friend at work?
11. In the last six months, has someone talked to me about my progress?
12. This last year, have I had opportunities at work to learn and grow?

Of these twelve questions the most powerful are those with connections to the most business outcomes. The first six are the key critical questions that determine the success of a company's ability to attract and retain the best talent.

The common link among these six questions is the fact that they all relate to what is commonly known as performance management. As managers, we see that our effectiveness in implementing performance management determines employee satisfaction, how committed employees are to their organization, and the level of their commitment to their own performance and productivity.

CHAPTER 2

The Performance Management Process

Consistently successful companies create high employee expectations, set demanding yet achievable goals, and achieve excellent results. They recognize that organizational execution at the highest standard is essential for a company to achieve its vision. Alignment of the workforce to those standards is crucial for success.

Managing employee performance at these levels is a key leadership skill. Performance management is the ongoing process and toolset by which a manager and employee first agree on performance expectations, and set measurable standards for achievement. The process also includes the ongoing support provided by the manager through feedback, coaching and counseling. Regular performance reviews, recognition and reward systems are the final step of this process to match rewards to actual performance.

Performance management encompasses the entire process, and is potentially the single most powerful tool for both motivating and inspiring employees to achieve consistent peak performance.

Performance Management Defined

Performance Management is the defined process for aligning organizational, team and individual goals, and for continually improving team and individual performance.

Performance Management is the ongoing communication process between manager and employee to establish clear expectations about:
* The essential purpose and responsibilities of the employee's job.
* What doing the job well means.
* How the employee and manager will work together to develop, sustain, build and improve employee performance.
* How job performance will be measured.
* How to identify and remove barriers to performance.

- What employee performance improvements are required.
- The short and long-term consequences of above standard, standard, and sub-standard performance.

Performance Management Process Macro Elements

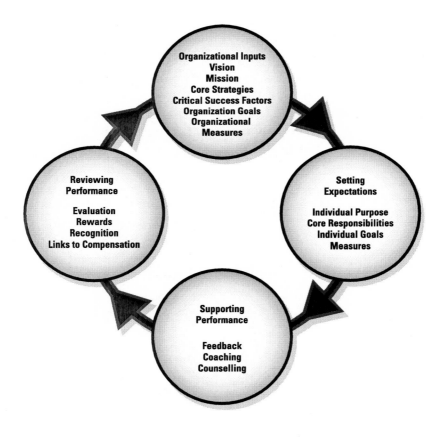

Another View of the Process

The Performance Management process typically takes place over a twelve-month cycle – coincident with the annual planning and budgeting cycle used by most organizations. Once an organization sets its goals for the upcoming year it is natural for those goals to flow through all levels of the organization, thereby ensuring employee understanding and alignment.

The following diagram outlines this annual process for individual employees.

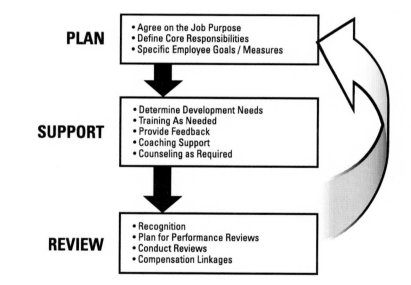

PLAN
- Agree on the Job Purpose
- Define Core Responsibilities
- Specific Employee Goals / Measures

SUPPORT
- Determine Development Needs
- Training As Needed
- Provide Feedback
- Coaching Support
- Counseling as Required

REVIEW
- Recognition
- Plan for Performance Reviews
- Conduct Reviews
- Compensation Linkages

Other elements related to performance management
- Job Descriptions
- Strategic Staffing
- Succession Planning
- Career Development
- Benefits
- Compensation
- Incentives
- Reward and Recognition System

Myths and Realities About Performance Management

Over the years, a number of myths have evolved regarding the performance management process. The following is a list of the most commonly held myths and the actual reality of the process.

Objectivity

Myth – If the process isn't objective (only hard numbers), it's not fair.

Reality – By its very nature, performance management includes both quantitative and qualitative elements. Objectivity is not limited to hard numbers. As long as several individuals can observe something and come to the same understanding or conclusion about it, it is objective even though it may not be quantitative

Ratings

Myth – You must have a numeric rating system to remove any bias.

Reality – Ratings are inherently subjective, and managers quickly learn how to cheat the system to reach whatever pre-determined conclusion they have already decided on about an employee. Managers and employees should discuss performance, gain agreement, and write down the agreement. Don't worry about a number rating.

Primary Focus is on Past Performance

Myth – The process is primarily retrospective, reviewing past performance.

Reality – Most of the focus should be on future performance, where agreements can make a difference. The past is only useful to historians and accountants.

Individual

Myth – The process must be conducted in private with each individual.

Reality – The process can also be conducted in a supportive team environment as an integral part of managing the business. Peer reviews based on positive rules of engagement reduce manager-employee conflict and increase the credibility of the feedback in the mind of the employee.

Formal

> **Myth** – The process must be formal with scheduled meetings.
>
> **Reality** – Once goals are agreed, regular manager-employee discussions should occur frequently and spontaneously, as well as in scheduled one-on-one meetings.

Time Consuming

> **Myth** – The process takes a great deal of the manager's time and reduces his/her time available for "real work."
>
> **Reality** – The process increases productivity because it eliminates the misunderstandings and re-work caused by lack of clarity. This is the manager's real work.

Principles of Performance Management

1. *The purpose of performance management is to reinforce and create the mutual success of both the employee and the organization.*
   - This is not a process designed to control behavior or play gotcha with people.
   - This is not a process for which its primary purpose is to drive compensation decisions.
   - The performance objectives for each employee must be tied directly to the business goals of the organization.

2. *Employees should know what is expected of them at all times.*
   - These expectations are a combination of both relatively consistent core responsibilities and frequently changing and evolving goals.
   - The process must be flexible and adaptable so that goals can be modified easily for an individual as organizational requirements shift goals to meet changing business needs.

3. *Performance expectations must be based on an employee's real work - their purpose in the organization.*
   - A performance management process must deal with the real substance of the business, and focus on real-time work priorities; not an administrative tool that adds paperwork.

- An employee's individual contribution should define his/her total contribution to the business. Responsibilities should include both the quantitative and qualitative results essential to the success of the enterprise (including such behavioral factors as customer relations or team contribution).

4. *The key outcome of the performance management process must be improved performance for each employee every year in his/her current work assignment.*
   - The focus of the process is to enhance and reinforce performance in the employee's current work assignment.
   - Performance management should not be used as a primary career development or succession planning tool. Career development and succession planning should be conducted as separate management activities.
   - The process should have a strong developmental component, focusing on improving the performance of each employee every year in his/her current position.

5. *Performance criteria are not the same for each person with the same job title or role. Performance expectations should be based on competence, experience and prior performance, as well as personal qualities that the employee brings to the job by both the employee and the manager.*
   - Not everyone with the same job title or job description should have the same responsibilities or goals. These vary with experience and competence.
   - Advancement through the various levels of competence in a job should be based on performance, not time-in-grade or seniority.

6. *Performance management is a two-way process implemented by both the employee and his/her manager together.*
   - Communication and feedback must go in both directions.
   - Both must participate in setting mutual expectations to create trust and support during implementation.
   - Employees should receive ongoing performance feedback to make course corrections, develop and improve performance.

7. *Performance management is a yearly cycle that typically ends with a formal evaluation.*
   - Results of the process are recorded, and contribute to the employee's future assignments, career development, and compensation.
   - The process is ongoing, supported with regular (weekly or bi-weekly) one-on-one meetings that ensure continued alignment and performance.
   - The focus should be on the future, not the past. Once an agreement has been reached regarding past performance, the discussion should shift to the upcoming year - how improvements can be made and additional value created.

8. *The organization's compensation system should be loosely linked to the performance management process.*
   - The results of performance management should inform the compensation process to the extent that it should differentiate between outstanding performers, those meeting job expectations, and those not meeting expectations.
   - It is not a tool designed to precisely determine or drive formula-driven compensation decisions or recommendations.
   - Salary-based compensation systems cannot adequately address significant performance differentials, and should not be manipulated in an to attempt to achieve that goal.
   - Compensation systems that are directly linked to performance management must have a true "pay for performance" element. This is described in subsequent chapters of this book.

9. *Performance management must be simple to use and administer so that it contributes to the effectiveness of both the employee and manager.*
   - It cannot be an overhead bureaucratic process that detracts from the real work of the organization.
   - It must be able to be implemented by managers as an integral part of their day-to-day work.
   - It must add value to the communications that should occur between manager ad employee.

Performance Management Process Linkages

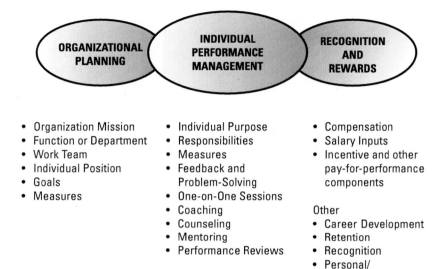

- Organization Mission
- Function or Department
- Work Team
- Individual Position
- Goals
- Measures

- Individual Purpose
- Responsibilities
- Measures
- Feedback and Problem-Solving
- One-on-One Sessions
- Coaching
- Counseling
- Mentoring
- Performance Reviews

- Compensation
- Salary Inputs
- Incentive and other pay-for-performance components

Other
- Career Development
- Retention
- Recognition
- Personal/ Professional Growth

Individual and Organizational Linkages

The Organization has:	An Individual has:
Mission ⟷	Purpose
Strategic Goals ⟵⟶	Core Responsibilities
BHAGs (Big Hairy Audacious Goals) ⟷	Stretch Targets
Critical Success Factors ⟵⟶	Standards (Measures)
Department Objectives ⟷	Individual Goals or Objectives

CHAPTER 3

The Magic of Performance Management

If performance management has such a high impact on individual and organizational productivity, and ultimately customer satisfaction and bottom line profitability, how does it actually work? What causes this tool to be so effective?

There are two elements that create the potential impact made possible through performance management. One is organizational alignment; the other is unleashing or energizing human performance. Let's look at both.

Organizational Alignment

Alignment is the process by which the vision, mission, core strategies, goals and success measures of an organization are brought into harmony in the minds of all employees through all levels of the organization. In an aligned organization, all employees know what is expected of them. They understand how their performance expectations are directly connected to the needs and goals of their manager, their co-workers, and the organization's customers. Even more importantly, they understand how their own personal goals and work objectives are linked to the overall vision, mission and core strategies of the organization.

When individuals are clear about their responsibilities and how those responsibilities connect to the broader organization, they are empowered to take the initiative in accomplishing their work, and they understand the importance and meaningfulness of their work.

Let's consider an everyday example. When asked about the word 'alignment' most people think about their automobile - getting an alignment done to the front end of the car. The process of aligning the front end of a car is pretty straightforward. Adjustments are made so that both front tires are both vertical – not toeing in or out. Then they are made parallel to each other so they are moving in the same direction.

Finally, they are made parallel to the frame of the car. When the process is completed, the car and the two front tires are all pointed in the same direction to give you the smoothest, easiest, most efficient ride possible.

Now, let's think about a car in which the tires are generally going in the right direction, but are slightly misaligned. The right front tire is pointed slightly out, so the car will make a right turn without your hands on the steering wheel if you let it. The left tire is on a slight angle inward, so that only the inside half of the tire is actually touching the road and is bearing all the weight.

Can you make this car go where you want it to? Sure! But it's not easy. The ride will be rough. You will have to fight the steering wheel the whole way to keep from veering to the right. The left tire will wear out more quickly because only half of it is being used. In addition, you run the risk of a blowout on that tire because of the extra pressure on a small portion of it. Your ride will be less efficient and you will consume more gas. The experience will be bumpy and certainly not fun. By the time you get to your destination, you will be exhausted because of all the extra effort you had to put into simply keeping the car on an even path.

That is a perfect analogy to alignment in an organization. If individual employees are not perfectly aligned to the mission, strategies and goals of the organization, they will be moving in a slightly different direction – usually with the best of intentions. So you will spend a great deal of your management time re-directing these employees' work; telling them what to do next; correcting errors; and re-doing what was not done exactly the way you wanted. Different employee actions can result in a mixed message to the marketplace and to customers. Employees are likely to be in conflict with each other because they have different interpretations of the organization's desired direction.

As the manager, you can force your organization to achieve its goals – but the ride will be rough, cost will be higher, the work will be exhausting and no one will have any fun along the way.

The long term result of misalignment is an organization that is less efficient, less effective and delivers lower quality to both its customers and its own employees. And these reduced results are occurring while everyone is well-intended and working as hard as they can to do what they believe is the right thing.

The first part of the magic of performance management is to ensure that everyone understands the overall vision, mission and strategic direction of the business. Employees must be clear about the specific goals of their department, their manager and their co-workers. Then they are able to develop (or receive) clear goals that are fully aligned to the overall organization. This impact alone saves an organization from an extraordinary amount of re-work and internal strife.

Energizing Human Performance

The second part of the magic of performance management is its ability to energize human potential and subsequent performance. There are four ingredients that create this result: meaningfulness, clarity, empowerment and measurement. Let's look at each one.

Meaningfulness

Of all the factors that impact human motivation, meaningfulness leads the hit parade. Personal motivation is the force inside each of us that ultimately drives our behavior and creates life satisfaction.

Our behavior is influenced by both external forces and internal drives. Externally, managers use both 'carrots and sticks' to attempt to motivate employees and influence their behavior. The most common carrots are financial incentives. The most common sticks are threats of termination. Both are effective – but only in the short term. They have to be continually reinforced and updated, and they don't last very long.

The more sustainable motivating forces are the desires and drives within us that cause us to behave in ways that we believe will enable us to achieve our desires. Of all of these desires, meaningfulness is the most important. It is the essence of the human spirit. Mankind has always asked the fundamental questions: "Why am I here?" "What is my purpose?" "How do I fit in the universe?" "How do I relate to my fellow human beings?" Man's search for meaning is at the core of his being.

The truth of this is self-evident. If meaningfulness were not central to our lives there would be no volunteerism; no non-profit sector; no dedication in the helping professions; no drive for invention, beauty, music or art, philosophy or religion.

Meaningfulness is created in the work environment by connecting every individual to the vision of the organization. That connection is developed through the alignment of the purpose of every individual job to that vision.

Every job should add value – to customers, to co-workers or to the organization. And the creation of that value must be perceived as meaningful by the employee. Unfortunately, we often assign work or short term goals to people and don't take the time to connect the essence – the purpose – of their work to the broader purpose and contribution of their work to the organization. The janitor in a hospital who is told his job is to mop floors may see this as an hourly wage for his labor. Another janitor in that same hospital who understands that the cleanliness of the hospital is essential to the health of the patients and that his janitorial work is contributing to the recovery of patients may feel very differently and have a very different approach to the very same tasks.

This is illustrated further through the following story.

During the medieval period, a large cathedral was being built. Cathedrals often took several hundred years to complete, so many of the workers on a project of this scope never saw their work carried to completion.

One hot summer afternoon there were three men working in the stone quarry – all cutting rough hewn stones into square blocks amidst the stones, dust and heat of the quarry. The first man was grumbling and complaining to anyone who would listen. "Look at what a terrible job I have. The quarry is hot and dusty, the work is back-breaking. I chip away at stones all day and I'll never see anything for my work other than the pittance I am paid."

The second man was doing the same work, but didn't complain. He was even smiling. When asked about his work, he said, "I am making perfectly square blocks so that when they are all put together, they will form a cathedral that will last for thousands of years. If I don't do my job well, the cathedral will not be sturdy – my work is very important."

The third man was also doing the same work. But as he was working, he was singing to himself, clearly enjoying his work and taking great care in what he was doing. When asked about his work, he said, "I have been given the great honor of helping to create a lasting monument to God."

The work of the three men was the same. The difference was in their perspective – the meaningfulness that they saw in their work.

All work that contributes to the lives of others is meaningful. Performance management must help every individual understand the importance of their work and its contribution to others.

Clarity

There is a game often played in organizations called 'the rock game'. It goes something like this.

The manager says to an employee: "Go outside and bring me back a rock." So the employee goes out and brings back a rock. The manager then says, "That's a nice rock, but not exactly what I had in mind." When asked for further clarification, he says, "Well, you know. Sort of like the one you brought me, but maybe a bit bigger and a bit darker." So the employee retrieves another rock, only to be told that this is not quite right either. "This is pretty good, but see if you can find one that's a bit rounder and with some speckles in it." The next attempt is still off the mark… and the game goes on until the frustrated employee walks away in disgust or hits the manager over the head with the rock.

Managers often unintentionally play the rock game with their employees. They assign work without providing the full clarity regarding the expected outcomes or how the results of that work will be used.

Virtually all the performance management and employee satisfaction research evidence consistently shows that most employees do not have the level of clarity they would like regarding what is expected of them.

The Gallup research revealed that the very first question asked by employees is, "What do you expect of me?"[5] Managers commonly make statements such as, "My people know what I want from them. I don't have to spell it out." Unfortunately, that is not an accurate statement.

Performance management requires that both responsibilities and the measures of success for those responsibilities be developed with great clarity. Although short-term goals may not be defined, employees can implement their work with precision if they are in clear agreement with their organization regarding their responsibilities and success measures. This is the heart of performance management.

Empowerment

Empowerment is a word that is frequently misunderstood and misused. When asked about empowerment, employees often leap to an explanation that is synonymous with authority. Let's look at the term empowerment from a different perspective.

The root of empowerment is power. Power is the ability to influence the decisions and actions of others. People who are "powerful" have influence over others even though they may not have any formal authority over them. Consultants are often powerful people in their client organizations, even though they do not appear on an organization chart, and they hold no official position. Their power lies in their ability to influence the thinking and behavior of those with formal authority.

If power is the ability to influence the behavior of others, then empowerment is providing individuals with a similar ability to influence others. How does performance management enable or nurture this empowerment?

5. The Gallup Organization. op. cit., 2007.

It comes from the clarity and designation of responsibilities. When employees are clear about their responsibilities, the measures that define their successful achievement, and are authorized to fulfill their responsibilities, they are also empowered to take the initiative – to take whatever action is required - to fulfill those responsibilities.

On the other hand, if employees simply receive short term goals or task assignments from their managers, they will not take any action other than what they are explicitly told to do. Providing employees with responsibilities and the freedom to act is the true source of empowerment at work.

Measurement

Imagine the following scenario. You're in a tavern with a dartboard. You've never played darts before. Someone comes over to you and shows you where to stand and how to throw the darts. They then give you 100 tries and tell you to hit the dartboard as many times as you can.

Now picture another person in the same situation. The only difference is that the second person is told to hit the bulls-eye as many times as he can. Which of these two individuals do you think will hit the bulls-eye more frequently? We know from having conducted this experiment many times (it's fun sitting in a tavern, having a beer and watching someone throw darts) that the person who is asked to aim for the bulls-eye will hit it more times than the person who is asked to simply hit the dartboard.

The principle is simple, yet compelling. The more accurately we can describe the bulls-eye to someone, the more frequently that person will hit it. That is the power of measurement. The engineer's maxim is, "You don't really understand something until you can measure it." The management credo is: "People respect what you inspect." From the employee's perspective, you might hear: "Tell me how you're going to measure me and I'll tell you how I'm going to behave."

We all live in a world of scorekeepers. Everyone keeps score on everyone else. So the least employees should expect is a clear definition of the terms on their scorecard.

Creating measures requires that both managers and employees translate responsibilities into tangible outputs. Measures may be quantitative or qualitative. They may be empirical or behavioral. Regardless, the result of a well developed measurement system is clarity about the definition for both meeting and exceeding expectations. Once the target is set and the bulls-eye is defined, employees will hit it with increasing frequency – and take their own corrective action as required.

When individuals believe that their work is meaningful they have clear expectations, are empowered to take initiative as needed to fulfill their responsibilities, and have a clear scorecard with measures that define success. There is almost no limit regarding the performance levels generated.

When employees are empowered and aligned toward common goals, the results are often astonishing. Performance management does create genuine, sustainable competitive advantage.

CHAPTER 4

The Bottom Line of Performance Management

Over the years, a significant amount of research has been compiled that provides evidence of the "hard dollar" bottom line impact of performance management. Performance management has historically been a hard story to sell because the difference cannot be measured directly – it has to flow through other variables.

Accounting systems do not have any way to include the variability of performance management on their balance sheets. Accountants can measure the hard costs of capital equipment, of salaries and benefits, of facilities and operations. They can measure the hard dollars of revenue for products and services.

But since they cannot directly link such variables as human productivity, performance differentials, customer satisfaction, or customer loyalty to the bottom line, they tend to discount these variables. Yet there is ample research and direct evidence showing that these variables impact organizational performance and profitability more than anything else.

What We Know About Performance Differentials

- The best software programmers produce between ten and one hundred times the output of marginal software programmers.
- The best salespeople generate revenue up to five to ten times greater than those of marginal sales people – and at higher profit margins.
- The best teachers accelerate the reading levels of their students over the course of a single year at more than twice the national average.
- This is true in virtually every field of endeavor – high performing individuals outperform their peer groups at step-wise multiples, not at incremental levels.

Some of the cases can be made rationally, even before an analysis of the empirical evidence. Following are some of the costs that can be associated with the human talent in your organization.

The Costs of the Human Side of the Work Equation

Hard dollar people costs
- Cost of acquisition of talent
  - o   External advertising and/or recruiting fees
  - o   Costs of interviews – travel costs, management time, etc.
  - o   Absorption costs – facilities, benefits, relocation costs, etc.
- Cost of employment
  - o   Salaries
  - o   Benefits
  - o   Other forms of compensation – commission, bonus, rewards, etc.
- Cost of separation
  - o   Severance packages
  - o   Management time and attention
  - o   Outplacement costs
  - o   Potential legal fees

Soft dollar people costs
- Cost of employee installation or assimilation and initial development
  - o   Initiation or orientation programs, management time and attention
  - o   Initial training and development – costs and time
  - o   Less than competent performance in early employment stages while still receiving full compensation
- Cost of under-employment (if performance management is not used)
  - o   Performance and contribution that does not match compensation
  - o   Cost of continued training and development
  - o   Cost of re-work or unacceptable work products
  - o   Cost of poor quality
  - o   Cost of customer dissatisfaction – and customer loss

o   Impact on the performance of co-workers
o   Impact on those who have to cover for underperformers
     and do more work themselves
o   Resentment and subsequent drops in peer performance
o   Impact on company culture and expectations

The Compelling Empirical Evidence

In recent years, a number of research studies have been conducted that translate the impact of heretofore "soft results" for such subjects as performance management and customer satisfaction into proven hard impact on the bottom line, and potential growth and competitiveness of an organization.

Following are a few of the recent research studies and the evidence they have compiled.

The "Evergreen Project" Research Evidence

This five-year study was conducted by William Joyce, Nitin Nohria and Bruce Roberson and published in their book "What Really Works." The study compiled data from 160 companies and more than 200 management practices.[6]

The core of this research revealed four primary practices that must be followed by an organization for sustained organizational success as measured by total return to shareholders (it doesn't get any more bottom line that that).

The four core practices that must be implemented are: strategy, execution, culture and organization.

The definition of the culture factor is: develop and maintain a performance-oriented culture. These cultures support high performance standards, which are universally accepted by employees. The key attributes of this culture are as follows:

6. Joyce, William, Nohria, Nitin and Roberson, Bruce. *What Really Works*. New York: HarperCollins Publishers, 2003.

- All employees are inspired to do their best.
- Achievement is rewarded with both praise and pay.
- Employees are provided with a challenging and satisfying work environment.
- The company has established clear values and all employees abide by those values.

"Reward achievement with praise and pay-for-performance, but keep raising the performance bar."

In addition, the following practices are followed:
- Poor performance is addressed explicitly and directly. These companies have the courage to remove poor performers.
- Poor performance in failing to abide by the values of the organization is as significant as poor performance in achieving task-specific results.
- There is significant talent depth and these organizations know how to grow their stars from within their ranks.
- The work that employees perform must be meaningful, both in their work and in their lives.
- Excellence in management includes hard work, valuing the dignity of work and valuing the dignity of every person.
- Recognition by management that positive attitudes breed high performance.
- Performance is defined not simply in terms of the quantity or quality of items produced, but also as a function of the customer's personal reaction to the employees.
- Stretch yardsticks are applied to both organizational and individual performance – they are built into the culture.
- Measurement systems compare the organization not just to its own prior year performance but also benchmark it against its competitors.
- These organizations constantly raise the performance bar.
- Empowerment and risk-taking are encouraged; bound by organizational goals and values.
- Compensation incentives are linked to the progress of the organization.

What difference did it make?

This research study divided the participating companies into four categories: winners, tumblers, climbers and losers. The contrast between winners and losers is remarkable. Over a ten-year period here are the results:

- Winners saw their money multiply nearly tenfold, with total returns to shareholders of 945%. Losers produced only 62% in total returns to shareholders over the entire ten-year period.
- Winners had sales increases of 415%. Losers had sales growth of 83% during this same time period.
- Winners had asset growth of 358%; losers had 97%.
- Winners had operating income growth of 326%. Losers had operating income of a mere 22% over the entire decade.

This research does not argue that a performance-driven culture is all that is required. But it does provide hard evidence that you cannot achieve these results without one.

The Bain and Company Customer Research Evidence

In 2006, Fred Reichheld published a book entitled: "The Ultimate Question."[7] This book describes a multi-year research project conducted by Bain and Company.[8] The research addresses performance management from the perspective of the value that loyal customers add to a company.

The research study divides customers into three categories: net promoters, passives, and net detractors. Their results provide compelling evidence that customers who are promoters grow a company, while detractors have a serious negative impact on it. They developed a customer satisfaction scale that provides one ultimate rating: the net promoter score.

Their measurement scale translates the results of a customer survey into three customer categories: promoters, passives and detractors. Passives are

7. Reichheld, Fred. The Ultimate Question. Boston: Harvard Business School Press, 2006.
8. Bain & Company. "The Ultimate Question." Ongoing research. See www.bain.com, 2007.

not counted. Detractors are subtracted from the promoters and the result is called an NPS – Net Promoter Score.[9]

The Bain research also describes the difference between good and bad profits. Good profits also generate net promoters. Bad profits are created at the expense of customers – contributing to net detractors.

How much difference does it make over time?

Net promoters are loyal customers. The Bain research study validated that a 5% (a small number) increase in customer retention yielded between a 25% and 100% improvement in profits. Their research revealed a strong positive correlation between increased Net Promoter Scores and a company's average growth rate over three years (1999 to 2002).

This result underscores a fundamental principle: happy customers are also more profitable customers for a company. How is this so?

Consider the unhappy customer – the net detractor
  • The cost for providing initial service is the same as for a net promoter.
  • But this customer generally requires additional rework in response to their dissatisfaction – this costs money.
  • They spend less money because they do not trust the product or service provider.
  • They only buy when offered a special deal so the revenue they produce is lower margin.
  • They are likely to leave their provider – so the money spent to win them as a customer is lost.
  • They say negative things about their provider. Each typical detractor will bad-mouth their provider to at least five other people, costing future potential customers.

Now consider the happy and loyal customer – the net promoter
  • They buy more products which generates greater revenue.

9. NET PROMOTER is a registered trademark of Satmetrix Systms, Inc., Bain & Company, and Fred Reichheld.

- They buy because they like the brand and are not as price sensitive – higher margins.
- There is virtually no cost of retention.
- Their service costs are minimal.
- They promote other customers to their service providers and generate more revenue through others with virtually no cost of sales.

This is interesting research about customer satisfaction, but what does it have to do with performance management? Plenty!!!

It turns out that the primary difference between customers who are satisfied and those who are not is based on how they are treated by that company's employees.

So employees make the difference for the profitable growth of a company not only through their own personal work performance, but just as importantly, through the impact they have on building a satisfied-customer base.

Because of the significance of the relationship between employee behavior and customer satisfaction, the Bain research also identified the employee practices most consistently found among companies that have high – and growing – net promoter scores. Consider the following example.

EBay is an Internet company that has enjoyed astonishing growth. The eBay website says the following:

eBay is a community that encourages open and honest communication among its members. Our community is guided by five fundamental values:
- *We believe people are basically good*
- *We believe everyone has something to contribute*
- *We believe that an honest, open environment can bring out the best in people*
- *We recognize and respect everyone as a unique individual*
- *We encourage you to treat others the way you want to be treated*[10]

10. The eBay Company. www.ebay.com

Perhaps the most fundamental core principle regarding customer satisfaction is measurement. The Bain tool – the process of creating a Net Promoter Score – is a measurement tool. It is based on the very simple principle that you cannot understand anything until you can measure it. And you can't improve anything if you don't understand it.

Employees will match their behavior to the measures that they understand to be important. Everyone wants to know where the bulls-eye of the target is located so they can aim for it.

The rules for a customer satisfaction measurement instrument presented by The Ultimate Question are defined as a set of principles. Every one of them has a direct translation to performance management.

- **Principle:** Ask the ultimate question and very little else.
  - o *Translation: Focus, focus, focus. Giving employees too many measures is the same as giving them none. A few key measures that focus on what's really important is a critical tool.*

- **Principle:** Choose a scale that works and stick with it.
  - o *Translation: Define the scorecard you are using with employees. Make sure they understand what's on the scorecard, who's keeping score and how points are scored. Then use it regularly and consistently.*

- **Principle:** Aim for high response rates from the right customers.
  - o *Translation: Set challenging yet attainable goals. Make sure the goals reward providing the right products or services to the right people – where the impact will be the greatest.*

- **Principle:** Report relationship data as frequently as financial data.
  - o *Translation: People respond as much to how they are treated as they do to what is being asked of them. Treat people with integrity and respect. Be authentic and honest in communications. Recognize good performance when you see it and provide feedback regularly. Expect – demand – cooperation among employees and role model the behavior you expect of others. And*

it is as legitimate, appropriate, and essential to value and assess relationship behavior as it is to assess hard task productivity. Individuals who drive results at the expense of relationships are net detractors – with customers and other employees. In the end, they cost you money.

- **Principle:** The more granular the data, the more accountable the employees.
  - o *Translation: Performance expectations need to be clarified at the level at which they can be understood, and either controlled or significantly influenced by the employee. And feedback about performance results should be just as specific. Basing bonuses on company profitability and little else has absolutely no meaning to employees who cannot see whether or how their actions impact company profitability. Company profitability may be the determinant of whether the bonus pool is funded. But how much an individual receives must be tied to specific measurable outcomes related to their own work or the work of their group. In addition, there is no performance if there is no accountability. There is no performance if there are no consequences. Performance, results and consequences must be explicitly linked.*

- **Principle:** Audit to ensure accuracy and freedom from bias.
  - o *Translation: People respect what you inspect. Make sure that you actually review the results of all the work you agree with employees. And have regular reviews – in the spirit of helping them to be successful. Measurements should be objective. This does not mean that you must have hard numbers for something to be measurable. Objective data is simply that which can easily be agreed by several different individuals who observe it. Behaviors are as valid a measure as numbers, as long as they are not simply general statements of subjective assessments without any behavioral validation. To ensure 'truth in advertising' the biases of fear of retribution for failing to accomplish a result; bribery; favoritism; and grade inflation must all be carefully eliminated.*

- **Principle:** Validate that scores link to behaviors.
  - o   *Translation: make sure that the measurement system matches performance for the desired behaviors and results. Consider the high school history teacher whose goal is to teach an understanding and love of history, but whose tests are multiple choice questions about names, dates, battles and specific events. The measurement is objective and completely irrelevant. This is a classic example of measuring what is easy to measure but not what is important to measure. Make sure your measurement system is actually assessing the behaviors and results you are seeking to achieve.*

The research evidence is impressive. Customer satisfaction leads to growth, higher revenues and higher profitability. And employee performance and behavior is the dominant driver of customer satisfaction. Performance management is the tool that connects employee action to customer satisfaction.

The Corporate Leadership Council Research Evidence

In 2002, the Corporate Leadership Council[11] was asked by its member companies to undertake a study regarding performance management. The request was driven by the fact that member companies were experiencing limited or shrinking budgets and resources. In response they were implementing an overwhelming number of differing tactics and approaches, which were all generating inconsistent results. Further more there was no compelling evidence supporting one performance improvement strategy over another.

To ensure a sound empirical base for its research, the Council surveyed over 19,000 employees in 34 companies across seven industry groups, located in 29 countries. Their findings were consistent across industries, employee age groups, genders, and all other identified variables. They concluded that the research identified a number of universal principles that impact all work environments.

---

11. Corporate Leadership Council. *The Hard Truth About the Soft Stuff.* Summary of Performance Management Strategy Research. Washington, D.C.: Corporate Leadership Council, 2003.

The Council defined performance improvement as the process of achieving the following goals:
- Steady, quantifiable improvement of employee performance
- Achieving better performance with the same workforce
- Achieving better performance with the same individual

The following diagram depicts this potential impact. Shifting the performance curve one standard deviation to the right will yield a 34% performance improvement gain.

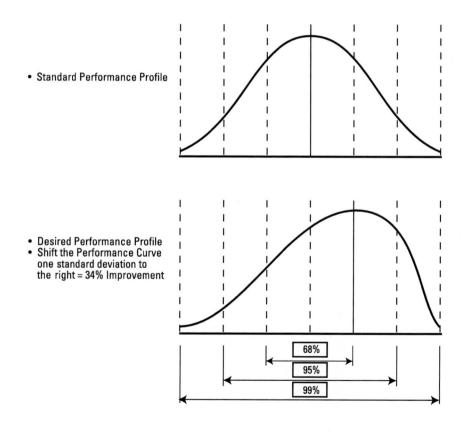

- Standard Performance Profile

- Desired Performance Profile
- Shift the Performance Curve one standard deviation to the right = 34% Improvement

68%

95%

99%

The results of the Council's research identified 106 specific performance leverage points. These can be divided into three groups and seven categories:

Organizational Factors
- The performance management system
  - o How the system works
  - o Clear definition of the performance standards
- Creating a performance-driven culture
  - o Cohesion (alignment) among employees
  - o Encouragement of innovation and risk-taking (empowerment)

Managerial Factors
- Manager-employee interaction
  - o How much managers explain what is expected of the employee
  - o How much managers help employees find solutions to problems
- Formal performance review
  - o The degree to which it emphasizes strengths
  - o The degree to which it points out weaknesses
- Informal performance feedback
  - o Emphasis on strengths
  - o Emphasis on character attributes

Employee Factors
- Day-to-day work
  - o Challenging (yet attainable) projects
  - o Successful projects (achievement)
  - o Earned rewards aligned to actual performance results
- Job opportunities (career development)
  - o On-the-job (OJT) development
  - o Actual promotions or expansion of responsibilities

The Impact of Employee Attitude on Performance

In addition to the performance management system, the employee's attitude also has a significant impact on performance. The following attitudinal factors influence up to 8% of the performance differential.

- Discretionary effort –
  The employee's willingness to put in extra effort.

- Organizational commitment –
  The extent to which the employee identifies with the organization.

- Job match –
  The extent to which employees feel their work is right for them.

- Necessary resources –
  The extent to which employees feel they can access the tools, information and resources necessary to succeed in their work.

- Team strength –
  The degree to which employees feel that the members of their work group contribute equally to the success of the group.

- Job satisfaction –
  The extent to which employees are satisfied with their job.

- Intent to leave –
  The degree to which employees are not looking to leave their job.

The Most Significant Performance Drivers

In reviewing all the data from the 106 performance drivers, the following nine clearly stand out above the rest. Every one of these factors has the potential of creating at least a 25% increase in performance. Collectively, they have the potential to create more than a 40% performance increase among the same employees doing the same job.

Top Performance Driver	Category	% Impact
1. Fair & accurate feedback	Informal Feedback	39.1%
2. Risk taking	Performance Culture	38.9%
3. Emphasis on strengths	Informal Feedback	36.4%
4. Employee understanding of performance standards	Performance System	36.1%
5. Internal communication	Performance Culture	34.4%
6. Manager knows how employee performs	Informal Feedback	30.3%
7. Opportunity to do your best	Job Opportunity	28.8%
8. Feedback to do job better	Informal Feedback	25.8%
9. Work for strong executive team	Job Opportunity	25.7%

Once again, the power of performance management is validated through empirical research – with impacts of up to 40% improvement among individual employees. Most organizations can think of no intervention – capital, technology, software, etc. that can match this potential impact.

PART II

The Performance Management System

CHAPTER 5

The Performance Curve

The performance curve is one of the most useful diagrams a manager can use with an employee to come to a common understanding regarding that employee's current level of performance, and the need for continued development in a position.

Diagram One – **The Two Variables**

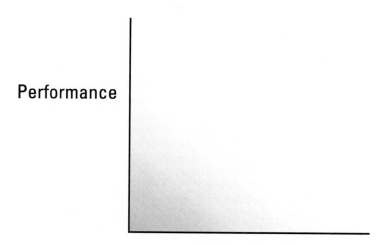

Diagram One shows that there is a relationship between the two core variables: Time in Position and Performance. All else being equal, it is expected that an individual's performance in a position improves over time.

Simply stated, we should be better at doing a job after three years of experience than in the first three months on the job.

Diagram Two – **Performance Over Time Is Not Linear**

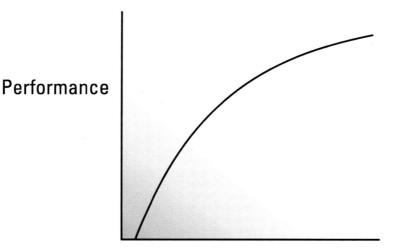

Diagram two shows that the correlation between performance and time is not linear. We learn the most improve more rapidly in the early stages of a new position, with continued growth slowing over time. There may even come a time when we have reached our personal performance limitations for a position based on our intelligence, knowledge, skills or natural talents. There is a certain competence level in any position beyond which a particular person will no longer improve.

Professional athletes provide a striking example of this truth. Very few athletes can achieve the performance levels of Michael Jordan, Babe Ruth, or Bobby Orr. Limitations of natural talent and skill create the upper limits of a performance boundary line. This is true for virtually any person in any position. At the same time, very few people actually reach performance levels at the fullest depth of their potential.

This is the natural evolution of any skill development model.

Diagram Three – **The Baseline Standard**

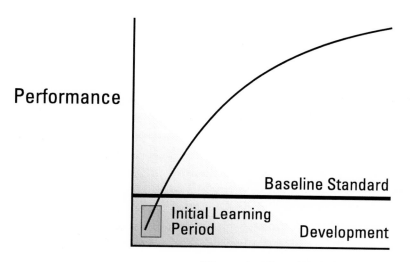

Diagram Three introduces the concept of a baseline standard. The baseline standard is the same for all incumbents in a given position. It represents the minimum performance level required for a position.

For example, if an employee is a trainer, he may be required him to maintain a minimum customer satisfaction level of 8 on a 10-point scale. If he cannot achieve this level, then he cannot keep the position. That is the minimum requirement – which is why it is defined as the baseline.

We hope that everyone we hire is at least at the baseline position for his or her job. Very often a new employee or newly promoted employee will not be at the baseline level at the time of hire or initial assignment. This gap is represented by the Initial Learning Period below the baseline.

When an initial learning period is established with an employee, it is important to define exactly what the baseline expectations are, how long the initial learning period may be, and what support and assistance will be provided to help the new employee reach the baseline standard.

This clarity accelerates the initial learning process and becomes a critical early identifier of a mismatch that may have been made in either a hiring or assignment decision. It is better to recognize and acknowledge such issues immediately than to let them drag on to a much more mutually painful conclusion.

Most companies have a 90 day probationary period for new hires. While not explicitly defined as such, this is an acknowledgement of the initial learning period needed to test the knowledge, skills and "fit" of the new hire prior to making a mutual long-term commitment.

Once the baseline standard has been reached, it is essential for the employee to recognize that the baseline is just that – a minimum baseline. It is not the measure of ongoing successful performance. The expectation is that the employee will now continue to progress into the "competency zone."

Diagram Four – **The Competency and Mastery Zones**

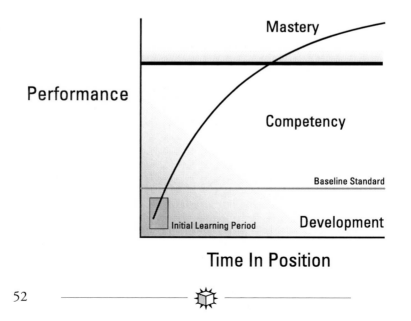

The competency zone, shown on *Diagram Four*, reflects a path forward for ongoing performance growth and increased competence over time. The expectation of movement along the performance curve through the competency zone is the reason why employees who have been in a position for a while are expected to perform at higher levels, and consequently earn more compensation than those newly assigned to the job.

The concept that competence is a range and not simply a designated point is very critical and often not articulated as clearly as required. Many employees have an initial negative reaction to this concept – perceiving that advancement in the competency zone is supposed to mean longer hours, or simply working faster and faster or harder and harder. That is not the case.

There certainly is an expectation of increased efficiency with additional experience. But often, performance improvements are qualitative – the ability to provide greater strategic inputs, develop new technologies or coach and mentor other employees.

There are many ways in which performance should continue to improve over time – as reflected in the variety of core responsibilities established for the position.

Specific competency growth goals should be established with every employee every year. They may be reflected in some or all of that employee's responsibilities. But in all cases, they should be both specific and measurable.

Many managers also establish stretch targets with employees as they progress along the competency zone. Both agree on what is expected, and then agree on how far the bar might be raised beyond these goals. Stretch targets can be established as the criteria for bonuses, incentives, or for identifying fast track paths to help employees who would like to advance their careers more quickly.

Diagram Four shows that there is also a "mastery zone" beyond the competency zone. Mastery recognizes that an employee has achieved the highest levels of performance in this position. Very often, continued growth once the mastery zone has been reached is defined in categories of developing and coaching others, providing cross-functional interfaces, strategic initiatives, process improvement, new technology development, etc. These are all examples of ways a job might be enriched both for the personal continued growth of the employee, and the continuation of added value for the organization.

If there is no continued growth or contribution once the mastery zone has been reached, the employee's compensation will similarly reach a cap. This is generally not good for either the employee or the organization.

The time it takes for an employee to travel through the competency zone is a function of the employee's skill and desire and the complexity of the position. It may be reasonable to expect that mastery can be reached for some jobs in a matter of a few months. Other positions may require years of development and growth. The expected rate of advancement should be developed by the manager and employee together, with a plan for showing progress established and monitored every year.

The intersection of the performance curve and the line that separates competency and mastery is often referred to as the 'ideal promotable moment.' This is a point when the employee is fully competent in a position. Growth has now slowed. For some employees this is a highly desired place to be and should be acknowledged as such. The master salesperson who does not want to be a sales manager but wants to exceed sales goals every year continues to make a valuable contribution to the organization. The master programmer who wants to continue to write code but not manage a development team should be respected for these desires.

For many employees the achievement of the mastery level of a position creates the potential danger of stagnation - no continued professional development or career opportunities. If this is the case, the employee is in danger of becoming less motivated (with ensuing performance fall-off) and the organization becomes at risk of losing a valuable employee.

For this reason, employees who reach the mastery level should have discussions with their managers to define their continued role in the organization, ensuring continued growth and contributions for both the person and the organization.

Diagram Five — **The Steady State Syndrome**

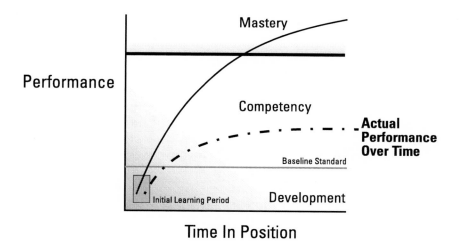

Thus far, the performance curve model shows a continuous employee development cycle with ongoing growth and development each year. Unfortunately many employees fall into the trap called the steady state syndrome. *Diagram Five* shows this syndrome.

These employees have established an acceptable performance level well within the competency zone. If asked, they might say something like, "I do good work and get good performance reviews. I expect to do the same good work this year that I did last year. And I expect to continue to do the same good work next year that I am doing this year. I'm a good performer. What's wrong with that?"

On the surface, this would seem to be an absolutely acceptable situation. After all, we all ultimately establish a level of performance that is comfortable for us. Why not?

In these circumstances, it is common to find that there has been virtually no discussion about performance growth along the curve. The manager sets goals with the employee and both employee and manager establish a comfortable mutual expectation and performance level. The manager has a good employee. Perhaps not a world beater, but a good steady predictable solid performer. The employee is similarly comfortable in the role.

But there is a serious hidden problem in this situation.

Diagram Six – **The Hidden Productivity Fallout**

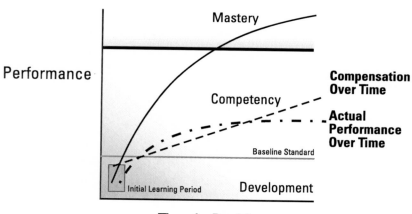

The problem of steady state performance is illustrated in the next diagram. Employees expect a reasonable increase in compensation each year. Some of this is a function of inflation. Much of it is a function of time in grade. Employees expect to get a raise each year and work their way up to the top of their salary grade scale over time.

Diagram Six shows that if compensation continues to increase over time while performance remains the same, an intersection point is reached in which the individual's compensation exceeds the value of the work provided.

Diagram Seven – **The Negative Value Zone**

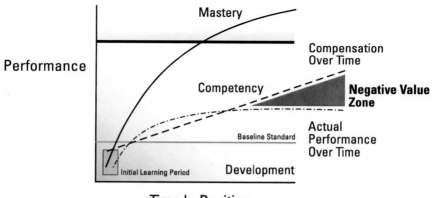

This gap is graphically depicted in *Diagram Seven*. When this occurs, the organization pays a disproportionately higher compensation for services than the value received, impacting organizational productivity and competitiveness.

We have all witnessed this phenomenon in large companies who typically solve the problem by providing early retirement plans with very attractive buyout programs to remove the many employees who have become overqualified and overcompensated for the value of their job.

These employees become candidates for early retirement or buyout packages if they have been with the company a long time. If they have been with the company a moderate period of time, they become very vulnerable as layoff candidates during difficult periods.

If the company does not address the problem at all then it has to charge more money for its products and services or reduce its profitability and value in the marketplace. In either case, it starts to become a very real disadvantage against leaner competitors.

The situation is not good. Unfortunately the problem develops slowly over time and is usually not seen or acknowledged until it is very deeply entrenched. As long as the company is growing, revenues are increasing and prices continue to move upward, the problem is not visible. As soon as business conditions change the problem becomes very visible and the solution is very costly and painful to all parties.

Diagram Eight – **The Desired Performance Model**

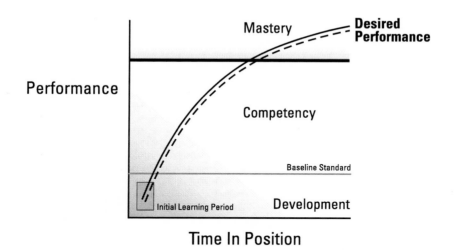

The solution is shown in *Diagram Eight –* the desired performance model. As long as we build performance growth with employees through clearly defined responsibilities and goals with specific measurements, then we are adding value to both the employee and to the organization.

The performance curve is a useful tool that helps us understand performance management concepts. Many managers share this curve with their employees, come to agreement regarding the employee's position on the curve (which may be different for different core responsibilities) and build annual plans that ensure continued growth, development, and performance.

Performance management is one of the most powerful tools in an organization's arsenal for increasing the performance of its employees and the productivity of the entire enterprise. With careful and diligent application, it can create a truly sustainable competitive advantage.

CHAPTER 6

Talent, Competence and Performance

Thus far, we have been talking about performance and the ways to advance along the performance curve. Many organizations have placed significant emphasis in recent years on competency analyses of positions, and built performance management systems around core competencies – at the organizational, positional and individual levels.

Competencies are often developed with multiple levels of difficulty and complexity, so that individuals can progress along selected competencies. For example, the competency "leads cross-functional teams" can evolve from the lower level of participating on a team through multiple levels of increased scope, responsibility and competence.

What's the difference between competence and performance? Can competence and performance be used interchangeably?

Competencies can be standardized across an entire company and defined in common across each position that has multiple people doing that job. By using different levels of competence, individual differences can be accommodated in setting performance expectations and conducting performance reviews. If competencies can be established as a set of standards with multiple levels, it is certainly easier to assess and check competency levels for individuals than it is to write individual purpose statements and responsibilities, as we will soon see.

The competency model has validity and certainly a great deal of appeal. Is it sufficient, or do we still need to address individual performance levels as well?

The answer to this question comes from an understanding of three terms and their relationship to each other. The three terms are:
- Talent
- Competence
- Performance

Talent

Talent is well defined and described with great clarity in the *First Break All The Rules* book by Marcus Buckingham and Curt Coffman. [12]

Marcus and Curt define talent as "a recurring pattern of thought, feeling, or behavior that can be productively applied." They emphasize the word 'recurring' – we use our talents time and time again. That's what makes talent so special – it is something that is innate in us and we use it over and over again. It is the driving force that enables outstanding performance.

Now here's the catch. We can't teach talent. We have to select for it. Once we have identified people with talent, we can develop it...but we can't put something in that isn't already there.

We know this intuitively if we take a moment to examine a variety of human endeavors. Once again, professional sports provides us with a great example. In sports, we understand that we have to find individuals who have the inherent capability – talent – the right stuff – and then we can develop that potential talent into actual performance through good coaching, practice, reinforcement, etc. We understand these same principles in the disciplines of music, art, literature, public speaking, and so on. The truth is, it's the same everywhere. If we can find individuals with the inherent talent to do the work that needs to be done, then we are already halfway home. If we attempt to build performance in individuals who do not have the innate talent for that work, then we are fighting a lost cause.

Our talent defines our potential – whether God-given or provided through DNA – it is the stuff that creates the individual potential within each of us. Whether that talent is developed to its potential is a function of our environment and life experiences. But we can't add it in if it isn't already there.

12. Buckingham, Marcus and Coffman, Curt. op. cit., p. 73.

The work-related message about talent is clear. Determine what types of talent you need before you write the job description or advertisement for a position. Build talent questions into the interview process. Look for previous demonstrated use of that talent. Remember that talent is innate and recurring – we use it all the time. If a candidate for a position can't describe any previously demonstrated application of that talent, then it probably isn't there and this is not the right person for that job. Don't try to develop talent. Hire for it. It provides the opportunity for excellent performance.

Competence

Competence is the translation or conversion of talent into the ability to perform. Note that we are saying "the ability to perform;" not actual demonstrated performance.

There is a wide body of literature about competence identification and development. The previously cited Corporate Leadership Council, a Human Resources subgroup of the Corporate Executive Board, conducted a survey of over 8,000 CEOs in 2001, and identified five common executive level competencies across industries. The competencies they identified are:

- *Doing* – Results, orientation, managing self-performance, accountability, initiative, innovation, customer orientation and persuasive communication.
- *Self* – Emotional intelligence, interpersonal relationships, personal credibility, integrity and continuous development.
- *Managing* – Planning, leading others, fostering teamwork, decision-making and controls.
- *Developing* – Empowering others, developing others, and managing others.
- *Leadership* – Strategic thinking, conceptual thinking, entrepreneurial thinking, establishing focus, influencing others, and attention to communication.[13]

13. Corporate Leadership Council. "The Hard Truth About The Soft Stuff," 2007.

A nice list. But very broad and subject to wide interpretation in use. In addition, executives could be excellent in some of the subsets within any competence area, while lacking core skills in other areas. This is a good start, but not sufficient for practical application.

Let's take the concept down to the next level of implementation. In working with one client in the engineering and construction (design-build) business, we collectively developed the following seven common core competencies. These were used with all employees, but defined very differently based on the employee's position in the organization. The seven common competency areas are as follows:

- *Business Results* – Ability to achieve desired business results.
- *Leadership* – Ability to provide direction, set strategies, align others, and build meaning through collaboration.
- *Communication* – Ability to speak and write clearly and listen effectively with understanding.
- *Commercial Awareness* – Ability to think commercially, manage risk and contribute to company and project financial goals.
- *Integrated Project Execution* – Ability to successfully use leadership, techniques and tools to deliver projects on time and within budget.
- *Leverage Technology* – Ability to apply innovative solutions to increase project and organizational performance.
- *Technical/Operational Skills* – Ability to demonstrate technical competence within discipline and apply it for project success.

Once again, these competencies are general, but at least tied to the project delivery nature of the business conducted by this company. Every employee should be focused on the delivery of projects. The competencies would then be applied differently at different levels.

It is worth noting that the description of each competence starts with the phrase "ability to." That's important. Competence describes our ability to perform – but does not determine whether we actually convert that ability into the day-to-day conduct of our work.

This next example is even more specific. In this case, the competency model was developed and applied to a sales organization in a company in the logistics/transportation industry. In this organization, sales reps manage a "book of business" of client accounts for a designated industry group or geographic territory.

One of the competencies in the model for the sales organization is aptly called "Selling." This competency is defined as: "A process of listening effectively, asking open-ended questions, and clearly defining the customer's needs and designing a solution involving the company's products and services, that exactly meets the identified customer need, then ensuring the solution is delivered on time and to specifications." That's a big statement, but it certainly has all the pieces.

This competency is then broken down into a number of smaller sub-competencies. For each sub-competency, a matrix of five levels of increasing complexity are defined.

Here is an example of the five levels for the sub-competency of "the selling process".
- *Level One* – Describe the steps in the selling process.
- *Level Two* – Help customers understand how our company's services can help them meet their business goals.
- *Level Three* – Create relationships with customers that result in buyer loyalty.
- *Level Four* – Coach and teach others within our company about our selling process.
- *Level Five* – Represent our company's strategy and services at the highest levels of customer organizations.

Competency models that are developed with this level of care, depth and specificity clearly have a lot of value. They require an organization to think carefully about what they want their employees to be able to do. The competency model can then be used as a tool for employee self-assessment, and for assessment by managers. It also helps in the goal-setting process for raising the bar each year.

The dilemma that remains is that if we only use competencies as the model for our performance management system, we are expecting that competence will translate into performance. That's a reasonable expectation, but it may not always occur.

Performance

Performance is the translation of competence into productive work. Performance represents the actual tasks and activities that people do – their actual performance – which should be the application of their level of competence.

If an employee demonstrates both consistency in work behavior and results, as well as a commitment to defined responsibilities, there should be a good match between competence and performance. As individuals become more competent, their performance levels should rise. This is consistent with the performance curve which travels through the competence zone.

But this is not guaranteed and not always the case. On the positive side, there may be employees who have some limitations in certain areas of competence but who are performing to their potential – even beyond their potential – through their personal drive, determination, commitment and achievement levels.

On the other hand, there may be individuals who are highly competent, but who are under-performing relative to their level of competence. They could do more or better…but don't.

This is why the performance curve uses both performance and competence. The curve maps actual performance against expected levels of performance based on an individual's position on the performance curve as they move through the competence zone toward mastery. Both competence and performance assessment are valuable tools, and even more powerful when used together.

If managers only use performance without consideration for competence, they may be over or under expecting performance relative to capabilities. If managers only use competence as their tool for setting expectations and reviewing individuals, then competence becomes its own reward – regardless of the performance or actual contribution made by that individual. When used together, competence and performance become a powerful reinforcing tool.

Increased competence should lead to increased performance. Increased performance raises confidence. Increased confidence encourages individuals to step beyond their comfort zone and raise their own bar to the next level. When supported and assisted, this additional effort further enhances competence. The self-reinforcing upward spiral of competence, performance and confidence creates a positive self-fulfilling prophecy. In systems theory, this is known as a "virtuous reinforcing cycle."

The reverse can also occur. Failure can lead to reduced confidence. Reduced confidence leads to hesitation, which hampers performance. Reduced performance causes individuals to withdraw or try less appropriate methods, which negatively impacts competence. The impact on competence reinforces further failure and the result is a negative spiral, known as a "vicious reinforcing cycle." We only need to look at the classic batter's slump that affects some of the greatest baseball hitters from time to time to see a vicious reinforcing cycle in action.

When managers see a vicious reinforcing cycle underway, they must intervene immediately. Managers should set a slightly lower expectation, provide help to ensure success, and start the cycle turning in a positive direction again. If caught early, this is relatively easy to turn around. If allowed to deteriorate, it can have devastating long-term impact.

The Normative Value of a Competence – Performance Matrix

The two variables of competence and performance can be used very effectively in a normative (comparative) assessment among a group of peers. The model shown on the next page is called the "Nine Grid Assessment Tool". Individuals are rated as either below, at, or above their expected levels of competence based on training, experience, etc. They are also rated as below, at, or above their expected levels of performance, relative to their competence.

The phrase "relative to their competence" is critical. A person may have extraordinary performance relative to his/her competence in the first year of a new job. If their performance level remains the same two years later, then the very same performance level may well be below expectations at that time, based on the increased competence that should have been gained through job experience.

By assessing performance relative to competence, we are treating newer employees appropriate to their experience levels, while seeking higher value from those whose competence may have moved into the mastery zone.

This tool can be used with individuals, placing each in his/her respective box in the grid. It can also be used for a group of peers, placing them all in one grid. This allows for comparative – or normative ratings – of a group. Some companies use a forced distribution assessment model in which peers are compared to each other. If the model is forced, then some percentage of each group must fall in the "below," "at" and "above" performance levels. By considering performance in the context of its relationship to competence, we are being fair to all, while continuing to raise the performance bar as competence warrants.

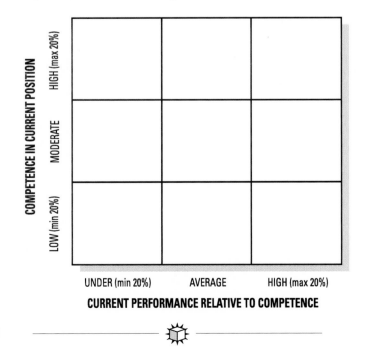

Each box of this grid has implications for the relative relationship of performance to competence, with guidance for managerial action. The following graph provides an interpretation of the implications for each position within the grid.

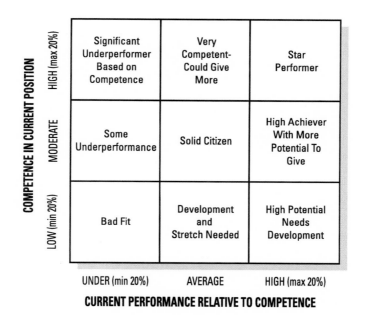

Talent, competence and performance are the three legs that make for a stable platform for energizing human performance to its potential.

- Select for talent – you can't put it in if it isn't there.
- Define the competence required to perform – and then assess and develop for that competence.

Translate competence into specific responsibilities and goals so that actual performance – where the rubber meets the road – is achieved.

CHAPTER 7

Performance Management Case Studies

Case #1 – The High Tech Company That Couldn't

A world-leading high-tech company dominated its market segment in the mid 90's, with a market capitalization of about 6 billion dollars. It had about 5,000 employees, with about 1,500 of them in engineering working on new product development.

After several years of market domination, complacency set in, allowing a newer, aggressive competitor to enter this market space with a different approach and technological architecture. In the span of one year, this company's dominance was shattered and their stock price fell so dramatically that they lost over 3 billion dollars in market capitalization in a twelve-month period.

This is not an uncommon story. What is so dramatic about it, however, is that it points out the painful consequences of the lack of a performance management system or methodology.

During its heyday years, this company did not have any formal goal-setting process – they didn't believe they needed one. Compensation was salary driven, with huge annual bonuses. The bonuses were not tied to individual performance and were issued to all employees as a percentage of salary. The company was so confident about its financial results that bonuses were issued in early December, so that employees could have the funds for holiday shopping. Bonuses became a standard expectation as part of compensation – an entitlement in the mind of the employees.

When the company had its devastating year, there was no money for bonuses. The employee reaction was outrage – they believed they were entitled to their bonuses. Shortly thereafter, the CEO was fired and the Board brought in a new CEO to turn the company back toward profitability and market leadership.

What the new CEO discovered was startling. During the very year of huge losses in both operating income and stock value, the following was also true:

- There was no formalized process for setting goals or expectations.
- All employees expected their full bonus regardless of individual or company performance.
- No employee had been terminated for performance issues – none at all among 5,000 employees.
- More than 95% of the employees had received performance reviews in which they were told that they were all exceeding expectations.

The CEO recognized that he needed to achieve a dramatic performance and cultural shift. Some of the initial elements of the turnaround included:

- A company-wide layoff of 20% of the workforce – including engineering.
- Layoffs to be based on performance – not seniority.
- No bonuses.
- Rigorous goal setting for the forthcoming year – at business, departmental and individual levels.
- A normative performance review process with forced distributions and ratings among identified peer groups.

What was the reaction?

- Employees were stunned and dismayed – they believed that they had earned their positions based on their years of past performance and the layoffs were unfair and unreasonable.
- Managers all agreed that among the 5,000 employees, there were at least 500 non-performing individuals – at least 10% of the workforce. Yet, to a person, every one of these managers then said "But none of them are in my department."
- The Senior Vice President of Engineering felt so badly that he personally interviewed each of the 300 engineers who were losing their jobs because they had been designated by their managers as the bottom 20% of their respective work groups. To a person, each engineer was stunned. They all had virtually the same comment, "But I just received a performance review over the past several months in which I was told that my performance exceeded

expectations. If my manager thought I was in the bottom 20%, why didn't he tell me so that I could at least have known my shortfalls and worked on improving them? Why is it only now – when I am losing my job and my livelihood – that the company is being honest with me?"

Over the next several years the painful process of creating a performance-based culture was established. The elements included:

- A rigorous goal-setting process at the beginning of each year to set measurable goals at business, work team and individual levels.
- A shift of the compensation system to a performance-based bonus structure, funded only by company profitability.
- A performance review process that included both an objective and normative component. Objectively, individual performance was assessed against goals. Normatively, individuals were placed in peer groups and rated in that group using a forced distribution system.
- Unacceptable performance levels were addressed with dramatic improvement plans that were either subsequently achieved in specified timeframes, or employment was terminated.
- High performers received significant bonus differentials, recognition and increased responsibility, and advanced career opportunities.

This system has now been in place long enough to assess its impact and results. To be sure, this company never regained the dominance it once enjoyed. Technology and market conditions had moved ahead too quickly for it to re-establish its position – especially with a large customer base using a legacy product with an aging architecture that required a substantial portion of the company's capacity to support.

On the positive side, however, this company is still a well-known, respected and vibrant force in the market today. It regularly introduces new products and has retained a strong position in its market space. A good portion of its stock value has been recovered and it enjoys healthy profitability once again. And all of this is being achieved with a workforce that is approximately 70% of the size it was during that devastating year.

This case study illustrates the dramatic negative and positive potential consequences of performance management and the criticality of its implementation before a major crisis occurs.

Case #2 – Accomplishing More With Less

This example is also set in the information technology industry – but in a very different context. In this case, a large bank had an internal Information Technology Department (historically called MIS). The role of this Department was three-fold:

- Design, build and maintain the technology infrastructure to support all the banking needs in all of its locations – including database protection and disaster recovery.
- Provide technology support for internal customers. At the Business Unit level, this meant developing new applications to meet business needs (either internal development or external purchase). At the individual user level, it meant providing end user desktop support, hotline help and training, as required.
- Provide the leading-edge technological services that had the potential to create competitive advantage for the bank. Innovative technology applications in this industry can create additional sources of revenue, significantly impact customer satisfaction and have significant cost-reduction potential through increased operational efficiencies.

Of these three roles, the last one clearly had the greatest potential value for the bank. However, this role could not be achieved unless the first two roles were being satisfactorily fulfilled.

Thus, the performance dilemma.

This technology support department comprised of 70 employees with differing skill sets. Of these 70 employees approximately 30 were devoted exclusively to infrastructure maintenance – server rooms, databases, networks, disaster recovery, hardware installations, etc. Another five were assigned to hotline desk top support for employees. Four more were "business relationship managers" for internal product lines, with their own small software development teams. After adding the miscellaneous managers, architects and administrative support, there was no one left for the highest value-added service of building or bringing new leading edge technologies to the bank.

This dilemma was further constrained by the unwillingness of the bank to add any more personnel to this department, perceiving it to be an overhead function.

To determine whether the personnel allocation was appropriate for the scope of work required the CIO, who was also the manager of this group, conducted a benchmarking study of other organizations of similar size and complexity. What he learned was that in comparable organizations the maintenance and end user support combined typically required 20-25 people. He was overstaffed by 10 people – all of whom were working continuously just to keep up with current demands. Something was clearly wrong. This was his organizational performance issue.

In conducting a review of the performance management model then in place, the following alarming facts were discovered:
- Job definitions and role distinctions had never been clearly defined. Many people were doing the same job – and even overlapping each other's work using different methodologies. Lack of role clarity also left some gaps that were addressed only whenever technology crises erupted.
- Work standards and methodologies had never been clearly defined. Such key policies and procedures as documenting change control and following technology escalation procedures were regularly ignored, or implemented differently by individual employees. The result was lack of knowledge of actual system configurations, crisis situations, inefficiencies, and lots of re-work.
- Poor performance was tolerated. There was no accountability. Poor performers were treated the same as everyone else.
- Because of the inattention to poor performance, higher performers were resentful. The consequence was a general reduction of work quality and workload. Individuals overtly made

comments such as, "Why should I work hard when others are allowed to do nothing and no one does anything about it?"

- The best performers typically had higher career aspirations and were the most frustrated. They knew what they could do – and wanted to do. But they were forced to spend the bulk of their time repairing lower levels of work not done properly. As a consequence, the organization had lost three key individuals in the previous twelve months.

As a result, the CIO conducted a detailed performance audit and implemented the following actions with his management team:

- Development and presentation of a definitive statement of the vision and business goals for the organization.
- An analysis of the current performance shortfalls and a definition of twenty-three specific areas that needed improvement.
- A meeting with all his direct reports to present these shortfalls with the clear consequence that if the management team could not work together to resolve these issues, the result would be an outsourcing of all infrastructure and end user support.

The management team "got the message" and accepted responsibility for the current condition. Over the next several months they implemented the following corrective actions:

- Business analyses to define all the organizational functions that need to be performed by this Department.
- Clear definition of the roles, responsibilities and accountabilities of the individuals who must fulfill these functions.
- A competency and performance assessment of the current workforce, and appropriate assignments of all to new roles, or affirmation of current roles.
- In some cases, several individuals were terminated. In other cases, individuals were given the opportunity to take lesser positions at lower compensation or choose to leave. Several others were placed on rapid improvement plans. High performers were given roles with greater responsibilities.
- Clear measurements and accountabilities were defined for all positions.

- The management team then established a feedback, coaching and counseling model that included a rigorous one-on-one feedback session with every employee at least once every other week.
- The compensation system was also modified so that bonuses and incentives programs were directly linked to performance.

After six months of implementation the following results were achieved:
- Overall organizational performance was greatly improved using standard measures such as system downtime, responsiveness to user issues, root cause analyses of issues, change control, etc.
- Customer satisfaction improved dramatically as measured by an internal customer survey.
- The overall number of people required to provide all infrastructure and end user support was reduced by ten employees. These positions were re-defined for higher level new technology initiatives.
- Some of these new positions were filled by employees who had the potential but had not previously been given the time or assignment for these activities. In several instances, key new strategic hires were added.
- Six employees left the organization – voluntarily or at the company's request.

Performance management was the tool that brought a hard working and good organization into a new standard of organizational excellence, creating value-added contributions to the business without any budgetary impact.

Case #3 – From Good to Great

This case describes a public sector Agency – a Sheriff's Office (Police Department plus Corrections Facilities) for a major metropolitan area.

The combined workforce for this Agency – sworn officers, corrections officers and civilian personnel is approximately 3,000 people. The Sheriff is responsible for the entire Agency. Working with his directors, he developed a vision and strategic platform for the Agency. The vision statement was driven by the concept of becoming, "The premiere law enforcement agency in the United States."

There is a significant difference between being "a premiere Agency" and being THE premiere Agency." The second statement can only be claimed and verified by one Agency. The challenge is daunting.

The dilemma is determining how to achieve such a singular vision. Here is the problem. Virtually every major police department of comparable size has the same equipment – same cars, same guns, same radio equipment, same uniforms, etc. They all hire candidates from the same national labor pool with similar credentials. They share information freely so they have relatively the same standards, same training, same technology, etc.

How then can one Agency create superior results compared to any other Agency? Their performance should be identical.

The answer is twofold. First, an Agency can develop and implement work methods or processes that are unique and superior to those of other Agencies. Work processes ranging from communications through dispatch; criminal investigations through community service; and internal operations can all be continuously modified and improved. Second, an Agency can deploy its workforce to create superior results through the combination of training, roles, responsibilities and active support in the day-to-day field work of its staff.

If all other variables are similar, the two leverage points for superior performance are continuous improvement of work processes, and superior performance of people.

This Agency established programs to implement both leverage points. A designated Continuous Improvement Office was created with the charter of developing a culture of continuous improvement. Its work included the implementation of programs to embed continuous improvement in work processes at all levels of the Agency.

Second, the Director of Personnel and Professional Standards (reporting directly to the Sheriff) undertook the design and implementation of a comprehensive performance management system for the Agency. Because many officers remain at the field officer level for their entire career, this became known as their "Performance Mastery" system. The concept was to bring the best practices of the Agency to every single employee – sworn and civilian – and thereby creating significant performance differentials – shifting the performance curve one standard deviation to the right.

The performance mastery process began with the analysis of the major positions that comprise most employees in the Agency. Purpose statements and core responsibilities with measures were created for each position. Responsibilities were developed at four levels. First, those competencies and behaviors common to all employees were established as the baseline standard. Second, those responsibilities common to everyone in a specific position, such as police officer were defined. Third, those additional responsibilities for a subgroup of this broader class, such as motorcycle patrolmen, were crafted. Fourth, specific responsibilities and goals for a single individual, such as training other motorcycle patrolmen specifically for parade duty, were developed with individual employees.

Using this process, a set of responsibilities were developed for every employee in the Agency. While most responsibilities remained relatively stable over time, specific goals could be changed easily and rapidly for individual assignments and special circumstances.

Once measurable responsibilities were established, all those who supervised others were trained in coaching, counseling and feedback skills to increase communications and performance on an ongoing basis.

The third element of the system (after setting expectations and supporting performance) related to evaluations and career progression. This area was somewhat constrained because salaries for sworn officers were determined through a negotiated union contract and career opportunities for both police and civilians were controlled by civil service policies, criteria and examinations.

Despite these limitations, modifications were made to the initial selection and hiring process to ensure that the best candidates were selected for employment. Changes were made as well to the review and promotion process so that the best performing individuals received the greatest promotion opportunities.

The Sheriff of this Agency has a statement that he uses quite often, "A community – a neighborhood - will only have the level of crime that its citizens will tolerate." A police force cannot prevent crime by itself. Nor can it adequately control crime without the active involvement and support of the local community it serves. Based on this premise, community trust is at the heart of the effectiveness of any local police agency.

The Director of Personnel and Professional Standards of this Agency described the critical role of performance mastery as follows: "We start with clearly defined and mutually agreed expectations between every employee and his or her supervisor. These responsibilities are described in specific behaviors so there is no question about current and expected performance levels. Thus the bar can be set and raised until performance mastery is achieved."

Once behavioral outcomes and goals have been established, supervisors can provide precise feedback for performance improvement, clearly defining what "better" looks like. This rising performance tide raises all ships, and every employee is expected to perform at continuously increasing standards over time. Thus Agency goals and objectives are achieved and continuously enhanced. This is how A premiere Agency becomes THE premiere Agency.

The result is not just higher performance, but higher morale as well. Higher morale creates a more motivated workforce. Higher motivation generates higher performance and a workforce better able to fulfill the Agency's mission.

Increased performance and responsiveness increases the public trust. Community trust and involvement reduces crime levels and enhances crime prevention. And that's what it's all about.

CHAPTER 8

The Implementation Challenge

With such compelling evidence, it would seem that performance management would be standard fare in almost every company, and implemented with great rigor. Yet, there are very few companies that have actually implemented or sustained a comprehensive performance management system.

To be sure, most companies can legitimately claim at least some elements of performance management. Many companies use performance management software to help support the process. Goal setting is commonplace and incentive programs are increasingly common. Performance reviews are often mandatory at least once a year in order for salary increases to be processed.

Managerial responses related to performance management often look more like compliance behavior rather than genuine commitment. If goals are late and performance reviews are only submitted after prodding by Human Resources, it is likely that there an underlying commitment problem. Yet commitment is essential for full system implementation.

Very few companies implement a systemic complete approach, and therefore get results that fall short of the promise of performance management.

Why is this so? The answer lies in one simple reality: implementing a comprehensive performance management system requires an organizational culture built for performance management. No system can be implemented successfully if the underlying organizational culture does not support, or even demand it. And that is rarely the case for performance management.

Let's consider the core elements of a culture designed to generate optimal human performance.

Understanding Organizational Culture

First, we need to define culture. In his book, "Organizational Culture and Leadership," Edgar Schein defined culture as "the pattern of basic assumptions that an organization has developed over time and become the deeply held beliefs that everyone believes to be true". [14]

These beliefs are typically held so deeply that they are not even discussed or explored at a conscious level. They become the unconscious psyche of the organization that drives overt behavior.

Because these assumptions are so deeply held, and often below conscious awareness, they are very difficult to change. Comments, even actual experiences, that conflict with these assumptions are likely to be denied, and even treated as threats. Challenges to these assumptions can lead to derision and even rejection.

For example, if a company has a deeply-held belief that customers buy products based on price, they will be driven to extensive cost reductions, position their products based on price, and engage in very aggressive pricing behavior with their competitors.

This assumption most likely came from one of two sources. One possibility is that it was a strongly held belief by one of the key founders of the company and was built into the initial structure of the company. The other possibility is that some early challenges – often at the survival level – caused pricing to be the driving force that sustained the company through this life-threatening crisis. Survival experiences become deeply imprinted in the psyche of a company and result in the assumptions that define an organization's culture.

What would be the impact of such an assumption over time? Product costs would be driven downward to enable low pricing. Pricing policies would be highly competitive. Overheads would be managed to minimize costs. Any frills such as attractive facilities, employee training and special

[14] Schein, Edgar H. Organizational Culture and Leadership. San Francisco: Jossey-Bass Publishers, 1985. P.9.

events would be minimized if not eliminated. Sales strategies would be price driven. The marketing programs would focus on price, etc.

Now what happens if a new head of marketing or an external consulting firm suggests that competitive advantage should focus more on a differentiated value proposition instead of price? One of two outcomes are most likely. The easiest response is rejection. The consultant reports are discounted, or the new marketing leader is quickly ejected.

Sometimes, the response is more complex. If the argument is sufficiently valid based on empirical data, or delivered in a compelling manner, it may be harder to discount, dismiss, or treat with derision. In these circumstances, the new ideas may be accepted – at surface level. But the first time the new concept fails to meet expectations, there are many people waiting in the wings to say, "I told you so," and bring the company sharply back to its traditional course consistent with its established culture.

This is why culture is such a powerful concept. It drives most overt activities – values, systems, procedures, policies, programs, etc. It also defines desired behavior and rejects behaviors that are inconsistent with the established culture. Yet culture is almost never explicitly expressed. The assumptions that define a culture may be buried so deeply below the surface that they are not verbalized at a conscious level, not even by those who most strongly live by them. They may even be denied at the surface level – while they continue to drive behavior and decision-making processes.

A Performance Based Culture

Most organizations state – and truly believe – that they have a performance based culture. Yet very few organizations actually do, creating the root cause of why so few companies actually have full performance management systems.

Following are the requirements of an organization with a performance based culture. These cultural attributes are described in their overt manifestations – so they can actually be observed and discovered in an organization. Following are these cultural attributes, along with the myths often held by management and the realities for many organizations.

Attribute – The organization is driven by a clear vision, mission and strategic direction that is developed and reinforced constantly by an aligned senior management team.

- *Myth – Our company has a clear vision, mission, and strategies that everyone knows and understands.*
    - o *Reality –* Many organizations have a vision that is ignored and no one can state it without looking it up.
    - o *Reality –* Most organizations that do have a strategic plan have to find it on request and it has little to do with how the business is actually conducted.
- *Myth – Our senior management team is fully aligned regarding our vision and strategic direction.*
    - o *Reality –* Many members of senior management have their own vision – often at cross purposes with each other. Functional territorialism and turf wars are common. This is not the measure of an aligned team.

Attribute – The company's strategic plan is driven down through all levels of the organization so that everyone understands how their work fits into the big picture.

- *Myth – Everyone knows our strategic priorities.*
    - o *Reality –* Most strategic priorities are not shared.
- *Myth – Every Function has developed departmental level strategies and tactics based on the company's overall strategic plan.*
    - o *Reality –* Most department managers develop their own goals independent of the company's overall vision and strategies.
- *Myth – Individual employees can describe how their work contributes to the company's vision and overall performance or profitability.*
    - o *Reality –* Most employees don't have a clue regarding how their work actually impacts the company's vision or bottom line.
    - o *Reality –* The goals for many employees do not align with the company's strategic plan. They may align to their departmental goals, but the connectivity to the higher level organizational goals is likely to be harder to find.

Attribute – Senior managers use the performance management system themselves and drive it down through all levels of their organization.

- *Myth – Every senior manager follows the system and has had their own expectations reviewed and endorsed by the senior executive (President, COO, CEO).*
  - o *Reality* – Most senior managers don't do it themselves.
  - o *Reality* – Most CEOs don't demand it of their direct reports and don't conduct regular performance reviews.
- *Myth – Every senior manager personally implements the system with his/her direct reports and then ensures that it is driven down layer-by-layer through the organization.*
  - o *Reality* – If senior managers do make sure their direct reports implement it, the exercise is likely to be one of compliance rather than commitment. Goals are rarely reviewed to ensure alignment through the organization.

Attribute – All employees know what is expected of them at all times.

- *Myth – Everyone knows what is expected of them.*
  - o *Reality* – The biggest concern raised by employees in virtually every employee study is, "What is it you expect from me? What do you mean by doing a good job?
- *Myth – Managers tell their employees what they want. There isn't any confusion about what's expected.*
  - o *Reality* – Employees may be given clear short-term goals or task assignments, but do not have sufficient clarity to take initiative in fulfilling their responsibilities.

Attribute – The organization has a clear goal-setting system to ensure aligned expectations at all levels.

- *Myth – We have a goal setting system. Here it is.*
  - o *Reality* – The system may be less sophisticated or established than believed.
- *Myth – Human Resources manages the system, but all managers use it as a tool with their employees.*
  - o *Reality* – Human Resources may administer the system, but it is completed by managers as a compliance exercise rather than as a useful tool.

Attribute – Measurement systems exist at both organizational and employee levels, and the critical success factors for the organization drive the measurement system.

- *Myth* – *We have measures at all levels and they are linked together.*
    - o *Reality* – Measures do exist for "hard" areas such as manufacturing costs and sales. Measurements often do not exist for "softer" areas such as customer satisfaction.
    - o *Reality* – Most employee measures are stand-alone for that employee and not linked to the company strategies.
    - o *Reality* – Most measures consist of those items that are easy to measure and do not include measures for areas that may be critical but not as easy to measure.

Attribute – Accountability is well-defined, understood and accepted by all employees.

- *Myth* – *Our employees know and accept their areas of accountability.*
    - o *Reality* – Most employees do not feel that they or their colleagues are actually held accountable for their work results.
    - o *Reality* – Most employees believe that the lack of accountability translates to little difference between minimal and extraordinary performance.
    - o *Reality* – Most employees do not believe that their organization actually holds people accountable.

Attribute – Employees understand the core purpose for their own position.

- *Myth* – *People know what they're here for. They know why their job exists.*
    - o *Reality* – Most employees can answer questions about the major elements of their job description. But they cannot describe the core purpose of their position.
- *Myth* – *Employees understand their core responsibilities and are empowered to fulfill them.*
    - o *Reality* – Most employees can describe their short-term goals and specific task assignments. But they do not understand their broader responsibilities – thereby limiting their ability to take initiative or act in an empowered manner.

Attribute – Employees have the appropriate authority and freedom of action to fulfill their responsibilities without being micro-managed.

- *Myth – Our employees are empowered to act. They don't exercise as much authority as they actually have.*
    - o *Reality* – Most employees describe their environment as one of micro-management in which their work is over-inspected with very little freedom of independent action.
    - o *Reality* – Employees find their decisions reversed, or are told to submit recommendations but leave the decision-making to their manager.

Attribute – Managers provide regular feedback and support to employees so they know where they stand at all times, and can improve in their work.

- *Myth – "I talk with my employees all the time."*
    - o *Reality* – Employees receive task-specific feedback, but very little else in the form of either coaching or counseling.
- *Myth – Managers coach their employees for superior performance.*
    - o *Reality* – Very little coaching can be found.

Attribute – The organization has a variety of recognition programs that genuinely recognize high performance.

- *Myth – We recognize good performance regularly.*
    - o *Reality* – Most employees perceive recognition to be very rare and only for the select few.

Attribute – Performance reviews are conducted with care and create an opportunity for feedback regarding past performance and a future focus for the upcoming year's responsibilities.

- *Myth – All managers conduct performance reviews. They have all been trained and it is something we do quite well.*
    - o *Reality* – Many employees will tell you that they don't remember when they actually received a real performance review. They do complete the form but feel that meaningful performance conversations with their managers are rare.

Attribute – The company's compensation system is based on and driven by performance.

- *Myth – We have a merit-based compensation system.*
  - o **Reality** – No salary-based system can adequately address performance differentials. (This will be described in greater detail later on in this book).
- *Myth – Actual performance differentials make a real difference at the individual level – in recognition, compensation and career potential*
  - o **Reality** – Most employees have a difficult time seeing the difference in how both under performing and high performing employees are rewarded.

Attribute – The company's productivity and profitability is tied to measurable differences and outcomes of the performance management system.

- *Myth – Senior management truly believes in the system and uses it for compensation and career decisions.*
  - o **Reality** – The system is likely to be implemented as a compliance exercise that contains "form without function."
  - o **Reality** – Even when implemented diligently, most organizations do not know how to link performance differences to actual productivity and profitability outcomes.

Why Culture Change Is So Difficult

Imagine a 52-year-old man who is about 30 pounds overweight. He smokes a pack of cigarettes a day. He does not follow a careful diet and has high levels of cholesterol. He doesn't exercise and has to take high blood pressure medicine. To top it off, he is pretty tightly wired, always under stress, and has a short fuse.

Not surprisingly, he has a major heart attack and ends up hospitalized. After some pretty serious treatment, he is given the following verdict by his physician. "You can live a normal and healthy life if you make some fundamental changes in your lifestyle. First, stop smoking. Next, lose 30 pounds and change your eating habits. Then begin a regular exercise program. Finally, learn how to reduce your mental stress levels. If you do all that, your body will heal itself and you can live your full life. Remain as you are, and your next heart attack will likely come shortly and probably kill you."

We check in on our patient about three months later and are very pleased with what we see. So far, he is following the doctor's advice. He has lost 20 pounds, exercises regularly, has quit smoking and is practicing yoga to improve his mental outlook and keep his stress levels under control. All looks good.

Now we check in again about a year later and the picture is not as positive. Our patient has regained most of the weight he lost, has taken up smoking again and his exercise program is intermittent. He has become a workaholic again and his stress levels – as well as his temper – are back to their former state.

Unfortunately but not surprisingly, shortly thereafter this man has another heart attack that kills him.

What happened? Why did these changes fail to take hold – even when the patient was told directly that he was killing himself? What went wrong?

The reason is simple, although the solution is more complex. This man made the right behavioral changes – but they were only changes in his behavior. What didn't change was his core value system – what he really liked to do and wanted to do. His fundamental lifestyle didn't change either. As soon as he removed some of the self-inflicted pressure, the behaviors alone were not enough. The change had only been skin-deep.

This example is a perfect analogy to the inherent difficulties of changing an organization's culture.

How to Implement Culture Change

The culture of an organization is like the personality of an individual. It is deeply embedded and very difficult to change. Most attempts at changing organizational culture are little more than speeches that describe a desire or intention, but have marginal content and marginal substance or follow-up. So nothing really changes.

Understanding how culture is formed is fundamental to understanding how to change it. The culture of an organization is first created by the founders of that enterprise through their values, their vision, their work ethic and the work methods they set in place.

Early in its life every organization is confronted by one or more survival issues. Crises of inadequate capital or cash flow, product viability, marketplace acceptance, customer concerns, loss of a major client, large scale system installation problems on client sites, conflicts between partners, competitive challenges, inadequate planning, cost underestimations, etc. are all common examples of survival challenges. Most young organizations fail one or more of these challenges – which explains why the survival rate of new companies is only 10%, five years after inception.

For those organizations that do survive the lessons that are learned in this process become deeply held beliefs that are subsequently embedded in its culture. The dilemma is that some of the lessons learned may not be appropriate on a larger scale or not valid for general applicability. This doesn't matter. They are assumed to be essential to survival and become embedded as part of the organizational culture.

The following case is a true story. A large defense contractor established itself during World War II by designing some unique technical solutions that contributed significantly to the war effort. For several decades following WWII most defense contracts were awarded by the government on a reimbursable basis. This meant that contracts were awarded primarily based on technical evaluations, as long as costs were reasonable (market level salaries plus fairly low overhead). The best technical approach typically won the bid. Companies competed based on technical qualifications and design approaches, keeping their cost structures competitive.

This defense company grew and thrived in this environment. Over time, however, the government contracting philosophy shifted to a model based on lowest price, as long as technical requirements and quality standards are met. Contractors shifted their approach to the design of acceptable technical solutions while driving costs downward.

But the culture of this defense contractor was so deeply embedded that it could not or would not change. This company's proposals continued to receive the highest technical ratings but it was not awarded contracts because its technical solutions exceeded the requested specifications. Consequently its costs were too high. It repeatedly lost on price. The company understood its problem but its culture and methods for developing proposals were so deeply embedded that it couldn't bring itself to change.

Ultimately, several of the major divisions of this company were shut down for lack of work and the entire company was forced to merge with another defense contractor in order to survive...in a much-reduced state. This is the power of culture on an organization.

The story of this company provides significant insights into our understanding of organizational culture. The combination of the founder's values and the organization's early survival experiences form the organization's culture. Other employees – even senior managers – who do not subscribe to these collective beliefs are quickly ejected.

Over time, these belief systems become embedded in the organization's policies, work processes, hiring practices, financial management, organizational structure, recognition and reward systems, facilities and customer practices. The culture becomes so deeply embedded that there is not even a conscious awareness of how much it impacts the organization. Simply put: "That's how we do things around here. That's why we're successful." Changing a culture is a very difficult challenge, particularly because the culture is so deeply embedded that there is no real conscious awareness of it.

Culture drives organizational behavior. Performance management very often requires cultural change. This is why it is so difficult to implement. Yet performance management, as a system and as a cultural change, is achievable. There is a methodology that can be applied very effectively to facilitate and support culture change. This process is described extensively in a separate White Paper indicated in the bibliography.[15] In brief, the process starts with the following distinct steps.

1. The senior management team must lead the process. Cultural change cannot occur as a grass roots activity in organizations. Neither can it be delegated to a mid-level management team. It must be directly and personally led by the senior management team.

2. This team must first spend the time together to discuss whether and why such change is needed. They must articulate what they want to change with sufficient clarity so that the difference can be observed and measured. This is typically crafted in the form of a vision statement with a desired end state that can be clearly understood by all.

3. The senior team must also define the boundaries and conditions of the change – what may be included and what is out of bounds. For performance management, such areas as compensation systems and incentive plans are often part of the discussion of what is in and out of bounds.

4. Once the vision and desired end state have been defined, an implementation team can then be assigned to determine which elements of the organization must be modified, so they will be in alignment with the desired vision.

---

[15] Resnick, Harold S. *Reinventing Your Organization to Achieve Sustainable Breakthrough Results.* Ponte Vedra Beach, FL: Work Systems Associates, Inc., 2002.

The diagram below shows the model used for diagnosing organizations and determining the quadrants in which change is required.

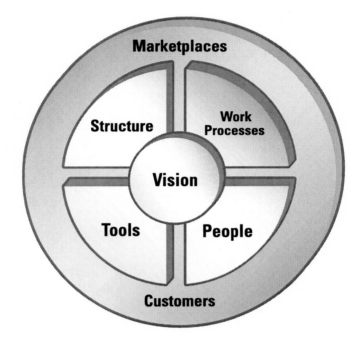

Changes may have to be made in a number of areas. In fact, changes must be made in multiple areas so that the elements that comprise the desired culture change reinforce each other. Single point changes don't have significant impact. As an example, mandatory annual performance reviews or insufficient by themselves. They must be part of a process that also includes goal-setting, feedback, performance support and recognition and reward systems. The result of a single point change may be a performance review process that is treated only as a compliance exercise, and therefore not respected by either management or employees.

Once the changes are made, the organizational metrics and control systems must also be brought into alignment with the desired state. Then communications and training can be provided that will be consistent in both word and action.

Throughout the culture change process, there must be continuous reinforcement – sustained over several years – before the desired culture becomes *the culture* – the unconscious way in which work is conducted, and the unconscious combinations of assumptions and values that define the norm of acceptable behaviors and actions.

Resistance to change is pervasive. If any parts of the desired culture are not aligned to each other, then the entire change effort is in jeopardy. If the change contains some aspects of the new culture and some aspects of the old culture, and they are in conflict, then the existing culture will prevail.

If behavioral changes are expected but the reinforcing systems are not aligned to require and reward the new behaviors, then it is unlikely that the change will be sustainable. The following chart shows how all the system must be aligned in order for the desired behaviors to follow.

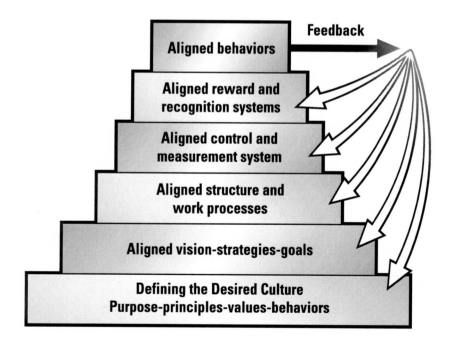

The Skills Barrier

In addition to the cultural and organizational issues required to successfully implement performance management, there is a skills barrier that must be overcome. Many of the skills required for performance management appear to be intuitively obvious. We expect that mature, competent adults – certainly managers – would have these skills and use them in the workplace as a regular part of the course of human interaction.

Unfortunately, that is quite often part of the problem. Many managers do not have the required skills and are uncomfortable with some aspects of implementing performance management – especially in conducting the tough conversations.

Following is a brief list of the skills needed at various levels of the organization to implement performance management successfully;

Senior management skills needed
- Setting a clear organizational vision and mission.
- Coming together as an aligned senior group (team) in support of the organizational mission and the core strategies required to execute it.
- Translating a vision into a set of clear and compelling implementation strategies.
- Establishing organizational measures – both quantitative and qualitative – that reflect the desired outcomes to be achieved.
- Implementing performance management personally – for themselves and with their own direct reports.
- Applying the discipline required to ensure that the performance management system flows down through the organization.

Management skills needed for interpersonal implementation
- Translating an organizational vision into defined functional (departmental) strategies, goals and measures that ensure the alignment of business goals throughout all levels of the organization.
- Developing individual purpose statements with direct reports.

- Developing a set of core responsibilities that have an enduring nature and that empower employees to take initiative in performing their own work.
- Establishing clear measurable outcomes.
- Providing performance feedback – both positive and negative.
- Conducting regular "one-on-one" sessions with employees that support the full range of responsibilities; not just short-term transactional work assignments.
- Coaching individuals on a day-to-day basis.
- Counseling individuals when behavioral changes are required.
- Conducting performance evaluations (reviews) that are useful, constructive, forward-looking and lead to enhanced performance and increased motivation.

Individual employee skills needed
- Translating their manager's work into a personal purpose statement and defined set of responsibilities.
- Creating goals and measurements that reflect all aspects of the position.
- Asking for help when needed.
- Soliciting ideas and inputs from others.
- Challenging existing work methods – taking initiative – when something needs to be corrected or can be improved.
- Receiving feedback in a constructive manner and acting on that feedback.
- Providing feedback to others – peers and managers – in a way that is helpful and accepted.
- Accepting personal responsibility and accountability for assigned work.
- Conducting honest and accurate self-assessments.

Some of the items above are skills, others are behaviors reflecting an openness in working with others. Both are essential for performance management to become part of the cultural norm.

PART III

Implementing
Performance Management

Setting Performance Management Expectations

This discussion about performance management would be inadequate without a set of guidelines to follow for implementation. Let's examine how performance management should actually be practiced.

Reviewing the Core Model

In order to discuss implementation, we have to take another look at the core model describing the performance management system.

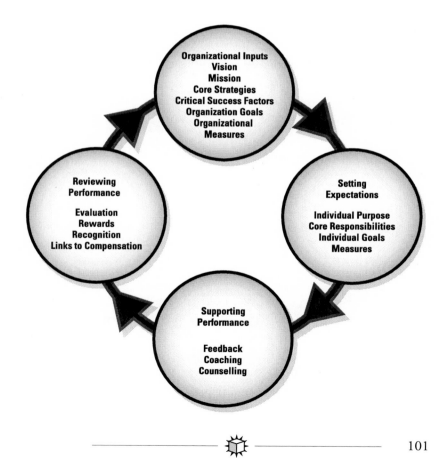

The diagram shows that the system has four major elements. The top of the circle – twelve o'clock – focuses on the organizational level. The second element is translating organizational goals and strategies into individual expectations, shown in the three o'clock position. Once expectations are agreed, the model shifts to the largest section in time – helping employees successfully implement their work, as shown in the six o'clock position. Finally, the cycle is completed with an evaluation or review – shown at nine o'clock – and the process begins all over again.

Setting Organizational Goals

As shown in the diagram on the previous page, the model starts with the top circle in the twelve o'clock position.

Individual performance requirements are derived from organizational goals. The senior team provides the leadership for the system by developing a clear vision and mission statement for the organization and the strategies to accomplish that vision. The mission is then translated into organizational goals. These organizational strategies and goals become the baseline from which individual performance responsibilities are developed.

But what if the senior management in an organization doesn't do this work? What if the organizational vision isn't clear and mid-level managers and employees don't have a clue regarding the strategies for implementation? Does that mean they're stuck and can't do anything with performance management? Not at all! It simply means that they have to take the ball into their own hands and start at their own level as best they can.

Under these conditions managers should develop a vision statement, core strategies to achieve it and measurable goals for their part of the organization – whether that be a functional area, a department or a work group. Managers must determine for themselves what they think their organization should be in accomplishing to help the company achieve its goals. Then they should meet with their own managers to get feedback and endorsement. This is the first step in the process.

Setting Individual Expectations

This circle – the three o'clock position on the diagram – has the greatest leverage of the entire system. If individuals understand clearly what is expected of them, they are much more likely to achieve the desired results.

Many organizations are very diligent about setting goals with employees, but they miss the greatest opportunity for empowering employees because the goals they set are narrow and short-term. So let's look at an alternative model and approach. The following model shows the flow of this process. Let's review it one step at a time.

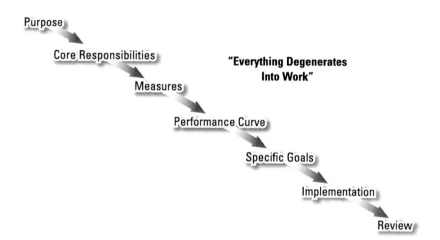

The Purpose Statement

It is rare to see managers begin the performance management process by asking employees for a personal purpose statement. When asked, the result is usually a blank expression. Yet a purpose statement can be one of the most empowering and clarifying outputs of the entire process.

Let's examine the power of a purpose statement through the following anecdote. Imagine that your organization was acquired by another company. The new president decided that he was going to have to reduce the workforce by 20%, but he didn't know which 20% to eliminate. He assumed that everyone was competent – after all, everyone received recent evaluations stating that they were all "exceeding expectations" (even though the company was losing money…ah well).

So this new president decided to invite every single person to meet him – one at a time. In that meeting, he was going to give each person one minute – sixty seconds – to describe the essential purpose (value) of their position. Based on their statement, he was going to decide whether he needed that position or not. This had nothing to do with individual competence or performance – rather it was going to be based on the value provided by that position.

In sales, this is often called *the elevator pitch*. Sales people are trained in their ability to describe and communicate the essential value of their product or service to a complete stranger during the duration it would take for an elevator to bring them up six floors. It forces them to get right to the essence of what they are trying to say.

Now let's apply this concept to a position. When asked their purpose, most people describe what they do. But the question isn't about what they do – it's about the core result or value that they are there to achieve.

Here's a personal example. A number of years ago, I was an executive in a large corporation. These were the days before personal computers, email, and cell phones, and only marginal use of voicemail. Every "respectable manager" had a personal secretary to take messages, write memos and take dictation.

I would typically go off to a meeting for a few hours to return to a desk filled with fifteen to twenty pink telephone message slips. My secretary had very efficiently placed them in chronological order and done an excellent job of recording each caller's name, phone number and whatever other information the caller would leave. The problem was that no matter how efficient a job she had done, I still had fifteen to twenty messages to return. It was pretty exasperating.

One day, I called her into my office and asked her the following question: "Miriam, what do you think your job (your purpose) is regarding my phone calls?"

She told me that her job was to do just what she was doing – take all the messages faithfully and provide me with complete and accurate information.

I then proceeded to tell her that she was doing the wrong job. She was doing it very well, but still doing the wrong job. In my mind, her job was to make as many messages as possible disappear so I didn't have to respond to them at all – didn't even have to know about them. That meant that I wanted her to listen to the call, solicit whatever information she could, and see if she could either provide an answer directly or refer it to the right person on my staff who could help with the question. In other words, I wanted her to learn more, to take initiative, to assume greater responsibility and to act with authority, leaving only those messages for me that I actually needed to handle myself.

Within days, my message level was down to two or three pink message slips for the same time period. Did Miriam make any mistakes? Sure. Did some items come back to me? You bet. But the overall result was amazing, simply because I was clear with her regarding the overall purpose of that aspect of her position.

Here's another personal example. I had a crackerjack salesman, Ed, working for me. But Ed was so focused on his short-term sales results that some of the longer term issues regarding customer satisfaction were being ignored. So, we had a serious conversation. I asked him, "What do you think is the core purpose of your job?"

"Simple," he said. "My job is to achieve my annual revenue goals at the agreed upon profit margins. That's what you pay me to do."

I said, "Yes, that is what I pay you to do. And I expect you to do it well. But that's not the core purpose of your job. The core purpose of your job is to make our company the dominant player in your assigned territory, based on both revenue and longer term customer retention and satisfaction. I expect you to create such a powerful sustainable competitive advantage for us that our competitors can't even get a foothold in your territory. That's your real purpose. Accomplish that and the money will flow."

Here was his response, "Wow, that's a much bigger job. I have to re-think what I'm doing and how I'm doing it."

Over the next several months, Ed started to engage in some very different activities. He stayed with customers through the installation of their products. He checked in periodically to make sure they were satisfied. He even designed and personally conducted some industry seminars in his area for customers and prospective customers. He created a customer user group in his territory to help customers learn from each other and make better use of their (our) products.

The results? Customer satisfaction went up, revenues soared and our competitors were virtually eliminated from Ed's territory.

Now you could say to me, "Sure, but you should have given him goals for customer service and satisfaction yourself. You can only blame yourself because you focused on revenue and ignored the other aspects of his job. If you had given him the correct goals in the beginning, then he would have done all of that anyway."

Now perhaps that's a fair rebuttal. On the other hand, if I had given him a series of goals, he would have accomplished those goals and then waited for me to give him the next list of goals. Even more disconcerting is the fact that I wasn't smart enough or close enough to the situation to know all the possible goals or activities that might be appropriate.

The essence of the purpose statement is to give an individual the larger vision of why he/she is there, and create a level of excitement and emotional commitment that says, "Wow, this is a really important job and I am excited that you are entrusting me to fulfill it." That result has the potential to create the internal drive that builds sustained motivation, initiative and self-empowerment.

Here are a few more examples of purpose statements that show how empowering this statement can be as the first step in the performance management process of setting individual expectations.

Example – Training Manager

Sample Purpose Statement (Limited)
Implement all established training programs, making sure they are logistically supported, and they achieve the designated acceptable levels of customer satisfaction.

Sample Purpose Statement (Expanded)
Develop and implement a training system that provides the technical and leadership skills needed throughout the organization to support all professional personnel, both in their current jobs and for their career development.

Comparison
The first statement will lead to a steady-state training operation designed to maintain existing programs. The second statement asks for a much broader vision and creativity in thinking through the job – possibly leading to alternative training delivery models such as web-based learning or mentoring systems.

Example – Software Engineer

Sample Purpose Statement (Limited)
Design, develop and test software that meets the required functionality and performance requirements for the XXX system.

Sample Purpose Statement (Expanded)
Design software modules as required to meet specified functionality and performance requirements for the XXX system. Build modules designed to integrate with other system components, while working with the software engineering team to maximize integration, operability, and robust performance.

Comparison
The first statement asks for independent work. The second statement asks for the same level of individual performance but also emphasizes the need for teamwork and integration with others.

Example – Sales Representative

Sample Purpose Statement (Limited)
Achieve your designated revenue, margin and product mix targets while maintaining designated satisfaction levels for all customers in your territory.

Sample Purpose Statement (Expanded)
Develop and implement a short and long-term sales development plan for your territory that will meet current revenue, margin and customer satisfaction targets, while implementing a longer-term program to establish our company as the dominant force in its market for your territory.

Comparison
The first statement defines the purpose of a high performing sales rep. The second statement asks for both a high performing sales rep today and a strategic thinker who will help build the company's future as well as ensure current success.

Core Responsibilities

The second step in the process is to develop a set of core responsibilities derived from the purpose statement.

There is a fundamental difference between core responsibilities and goals. As managers, we want employees to be responsible and accountable. As parents, we want our children to be responsible for their actions as well. Accepting personal responsibility for our behaviors and the consequences of our behaviors is a fundamental value system deeply embedded in our society. Yet much of what we do in the work environment is actually counter-productive to developing full responsibility and accountability in others.

Responsibility translates to results or outcomes. Think about your personal responsibilities. If you are responsible for something, then it is your role to achieve an output – a result for which you are held accountable – by yourself or through others. In order to fulfill this responsibility, you have to determine what goals should be established and how to achieve those goals. If you are not being successful then you need to modify your goals or actions to fulfill your responsibilities. This requires a higher level of thinking and commitment than simply defining or achieving specific assigned goals.

For example, think about our role as parents and how we attempt to build responsibility in our children. When our children are young, we want them to take responsibility for their own rooms. We start by giving them directions. "Make your bed every morning. Pick up your clothes. Put your toys away where they belong." The nature of the relationship is authoritarian and we expect obedience.

Then we move to the next level. We agree to some specific goals with related rewards. "If you make your bed every morning for the next week without being told, we'll take you to that movie you want to see." "If you pick up your stuff every day for a month you can have this special treat." We are now setting specific goals with our children, along with related rewards and negative consequences. This is certainly better than directing our children to perform the tasks we assign them. But the goals are still specific and relatively short-term. In our role as parents we set the goals and consequences, often with some negotiation along the way.

This is not very different from the way managers typically set goals with their employees. Either the manager or the employee creates the first list – then there is some negotiation and finally (hopefully), some agreement. Rewards and negative consequences are defined. And then the employee works to achieve the goals and the process starts all over again.

But the process is time specific. The goals are achieved or not and then new goals are set. If the manager sets the goals then the manager has to be smart enough and knowledgeable enough to know all the areas needing goals, keep track of progress and ensure the goals are achieved.

Let's go back to our children and their responsibility for maintaining their room. Using the goal-setting model we set and agree on some goals. We set goals for making the bed, for putting things away, for putting dirty clothes in the laundry basket. Then we come up one day and see that the carpet is filthy and hasn't been vacuumed for weeks. So we say, "Hey, you were supposed to keep your room clean. The carpet is filthy." And your child says, "But that wasn't on the list. I make my bed, put my dirty clothes in the basket and put my stuff away. You never said anything about vacuuming the carpet."

Technically, your child is right. You didn't think about it when you made up the list of goals. So your child accepted the goals you provided…but something was still missing.

What you really want is for your child to accept responsibility for his or her room. You want your child to feel responsible for the room, take pride in the way it is kept, and accept accountability for keeping it that way. If you could agree on that responsibility, then it is up to your child to understand and establish the goals – or elements – of what it means to fulfill that responsibility.

As our children grow and develop, we want them to accept responsibility for their interpersonal relationships, for their education, for their own financial well-being, for their lives as responsible, capable adults. Setting specific goals for them – or with them – will never achieve that result. We have to get past the specific goals and come to a greater understanding about personal responsibility. The specific goals will flow from those responsibilities.

I recently had the pleasure of a conversation with one of my own grown children, who told me that she was putting together her own financial management program so that she would be able to retire at a certain age having achieved her desired lifestyle. Then she told me how she was working with a financial advisor, investing in her 401K, setting up a savings plan, etc. She was developing her own goals based on her acceptance of personal responsibility for her own long-term financial well-being.

Now let's return to the work environment and translate this concept into responsibilities for employees as they strive to fulfill the purpose of their job. The fundamental question that managers should ask of an employee is, "Now that we have agreed on the purpose of your job, what are the areas or functions you must be responsible for to fulfill this core purpose?"

The answer should result in a set of sustaining responsibilities – usually about ten or fifteen of them. Some of them might be quite specific with specific measures. Some may not yet have measures or specific time-dated outcomes.

But specific goals or measures can be developed that demonstrate whether each responsibility was or wasn't fulfilled.

Let's look at a few examples. Once again, I'll provide a personal story.

One of my clients was deeply committed to continuous improvement as a core internal strategy for the ongoing enhancement of internal operations, increased customer satisfaction and improved productivity. This client recognized that continuous improvement would reduce the internal *leakage* caused by errors, re-work and inefficiencies, and would also result in increased performance and profitability.

The client employed an individual to provide the internal leadership for this effort. Since this was a new position, – and fairly general – it was hard for this person to get her arms around the whole job. Initial efforts were pretty tactical – improve this specific process, make sure our ISO documentation is up-to-date, etc. Individual results were okay, but there was no sense of a comprehensive approach to the role.

So we worked together to develop the role using the performance management model described. After about an hour of discussion with this individual and her manager, we agreed on the following Purpose Statement: "Guide the organization's continuous improvement system for the betterment of the company as a whole."

Now that's a big statement! It almost felt overwhelming to her. But it was clearly very important and very empowering as well.

From that purpose we developed the following core responsibilities:

- Identify core work processes in need of improvement, guiding Process Action Teams (PATs) – or other appropriate vehicles – to achieve those improvements.
- Maintain the ISO certification system so that ISO documentation remains current, and work processes and measures achieve all desired requirements.
- Ensure that the company's measurement system includes all core work processes, and that the measures (results) meet the ISO standards.
- Develop organizational competence and a sense of urgency in continuous improvement as demonstrated through PATs and other continuous improvement efforts initiated independently by departmental managers.
- Design and implement the training and other related support tools needed to develop process improvement skills throughout the organization.
- Personally coach and support PAT facilitators as needed to ensure the success of their initiatives.
- Maintain a continuous improvement (CI) monitoring and measurement system to document and monitor the CI activities and the tangible improvements achieved through CI initiatives.
- Ensure that the company's customer satisfaction surveys are integrally linked into both the cross-functional work process initiatives and the company's measurement system.

Now, the company could have taken a completely different approach. It could have said, "Generate one million dollars in savings or cost reductions for next year." That would have been a specific goal and the person receiving it would have been driven to achieve it. But achieving that goal might well have been at the expense of some critical longer term issues – such as customer satisfaction or improved product quality. Identifying all the responsibilities in their entirety ensures a comprehensive understanding of the whole job.

By defining the higher level sustaining responsibilities, this person can now establish a set of goals with specific measures that will define her job for the upcoming year.

In subsequent years, there might be some changes in responsibilities. But typically responsibilities have an enduring nature, while specific goals and tactics tend to be modified significantly over time.

Note that each one of the responsibilities cited on the previous page is focused on a result. The result may not be specific (requiring specific goals or measures) but a result is embedded in every responsibility statement.

From such a set of responsibilities, managers can proceed to the major discussion question with their employees, "How will you know that you have successfully fulfilled this responsibility this year?" This question enables managers and employees to look at every responsibility together, and develop a set of measures – or goals and measures – that they agree represent the successful fulfillment of those responsibilities for the upcoming year.

Following are examples of a set of responsibilities for several different types of positions.

Example – Training Manager

Purpose Statement

    Develop and implement a training system that provides the technical and leadership skills needed throughout the engineering organization to support the professional personnel, both in their current jobs and for their career development.

Core Responsibilities
- Conduct a needs analysis of all professional employees and categories of employees to determine training and development requirements.
- Design training programs and develop program materials as required to meet these needs.

- Deliver all training programs (personally, with internal personnel, or with outside vendors as required) to meet the training needs identified.
- Establish and implement a customer feedback system and ensure that all training programs attain the specified levels of satisfaction.
- Manage all training administration including budgets, facilities, logistics, scheduling, registration, and operations.
- Monitor program enrollment and attendance, making adjustments as required to ensure best utilization of the company's training resources.
- Select vendors as required, for training content and delivery, and manage and evaluate their performance.
- Explore alternative training delivery methods and technologies, and provide a set of recommendations, plan and budget for the use of alternative delivery systems.

Discussion

Note that the eight responsibilities above could be broken down into a very large number of specific goals. Also, note the absence of identified measures for these responsibilities. This is the next step in the process. But by defining and reviewing these responsibilities, this training manager is empowered to take the initiative in determining what is required to achieve the purpose of his job and how to satisfy these responsibilities. If there were no agreed upon responsibilities, this training manager might simply continue to implement existing courses, believing that this was the scope of his job and that he did not have permission to take on projects or activities beyond that scope.

Example – Software Engineer

Purpose Statement

Design software modules as required to meet specified functionality and performance requirements for the XXX system. Build modules designed to integrate with other system components, while working with the software engineering team to maximize integration, operability and robust performance.

Core Responsibilities

- Translate requirements and specifications provided into software functionality and design, conduct design reviews, write the software code for the accepted designs, and conduct unit tests for all software developed, ensuring it meets functionality and performance requirements.
- Maintain ongoing responsibility and accountability for all software developed through its lifecycle, addressing functionality or performance issues, bug fixes, and customer interfaces as required to resolve problems.
- Participate as a full team member for all multiple developer software projects.
- Provide project management leadership as assigned for any software projects assigned to you as the lead person for functionality, schedule, and budget.
- Serve as the primary interface for your assigned software projects with the other parts of the organization, e.g. documentation, software support and quality assurance.
- Develop new processes/methods to reduce the software development cycle.
- Explore new technologies and tools for iterative software development methods and provide recommendations regarding their use in our organization.
- Provide mentoring and coaching for new hires assigned to you for their initial installation into our organization, at least until they are able to work independently.
- Identify and participate in an agreed self-development program to enhance your leadership skills for potential future roles in this organization.

Discussion

The first several responsibilities reflect the traditional software development role. Responsibilities three and four address interpersonal and leadership roles. Responsibilities six and seven reflect conceptual thinking and forward-looking assignments. The final two responsibilities address development of self and others. By developing this broader set of responsibilities the employee is encouraged to take more initiative and think about activities that she might not have otherwise considered.

Example – Sales Representative

Purpose Statement

Develop and implement a short and long-term sales development plan for your territory that will meet current revenue, margin and customer satisfaction targets, while constructing a longer-term program to establish our company as the dominant force in its market for your territory.

Core Responsibilities

- Develop and implement a territory plan that will achieve the annual desired revenue, product mix and margins established for this territory.
- Implement your territory plan, making adjustments as required based on shifts in the marketplace and new challenges or opportunities.
- Participate in the sales prospecting and sales management process, providing information, feedback and guidance as requested. Provide inputs regarding how these processes might be improved.
- Develop a longer-term (3-year) plan to expand our presence in your territory, establishing our company as the dominant force for our product/service mix.
- Serve as one of three beta test sites for the New Systems Product to be field tested this year.
- Continue with the development of your own product knowledge and sales skills, participating in at least ten days of training during the course of the year.
- Provide marketing perspectives, customer needs and competitive information as required in the sales rep input program.
- Participate fully as a team member of your sales region, engaging in activities and efforts as planned to achieve the overall goals of the region.
- Support trade show and regional seminar activities as requested.

Discussion

Sales reps are, quite appropriately, short-term focused on their sales goals. But they also have a longer-term strategic responsibility, as well as the responsibility to contribute to the broader marketing and sales activities of the entire organization. The responsibilities listed on the previous page reflect that broader role. Responsibility number five (product beta testing) is a good example of a need that might be required for one year, but not for subsequent years. Softer responsibilities such as marketing input, team participation, and self-development are reflected as well in this listing of core responsibilities.

Understanding Goals and Measures

Goals and measures are discussed together because there are times when they are interchangeable. A goal is a tangible result. The measure determines whether that goal was achieved. For example, the goal might be to arrive on time. The measure is: within five minutes of schedule.

A goal defines a specific outcome or result. Goals are usually achieved by a specific date and must be measurable in order to be able to determine whether they have been achieved or not.

General statements used as goals are literally worthless.
- "My goal is to become a better person."
- "I am giving you the goal of being a better team member."
- "My goal is to fully understand our new software system."

These are all statements of intent developed by ourselves or imposed on us by others. Unless they are translated into specific, measurable outcomes, they are not very useful.

As a general guide, goals must be:
- Specific – there should be no question about what is being asked.
- Measurable – sufficiently specific so that several parties can easily agree that the goal was or was not achieved.
- Applicable – derived from a specific responsibility and appropriate to the fulfillment of that responsibility.

- Achievable – challenging, but not so challenging that it is not achievable in the mind of the person who has the goal. Goals that are set too low are not a challenge. Goals that are set too high encourage the other person to simply give up.
- Timely – goals should have a time by which they are to be achieved.

The difficulty that most people have in setting specific goals is not in creating the goal itself, but in developing an acceptable measure for a goal. Goals that are hard to measure tend to be excluded not because they are less important, but simply because it is harder to develop clear measures. Thus, we are left with a set of specific goals that are tangible but may leave out some very critical aspects of the position that require more qualitative assessments.

The following anecdote may help bring this to life. Imagine a high school history teacher who loves her job. When you ask her why she loves to teach history, she makes statements like, "We have to understand the past so we don't repeat it," and, "Helping young students understand history gives them a sense of their culture and their heritage."

These are laudable goals and reveal her passion for her work.

Then we look at her measurement system – the tests she gives her students. The exams are multiple choice, and they're all about correctly identifying names, people, battles and dates. What is the relevance of knowing the date the Battle of Waterloo was fought in light of her vision of developing a deep appreciation of history? Actually, very little.

How did this happen? It was the consequence of the measurement challenge. Names and dates are easy to measure. Getting names and dates and places correct on a multiple choice exam is absolutely objective. Assessing whether a student understands the relevance and relationship of major historical events to their lives today is much more difficult . So we tend to measure what is easy to measure, not necessarily what is important to measure.

There are several ways to identify measures for all responsibilities and all goals – and it is actually much easier than most people think.

I Don't Know How to Measure It, But I Know It When I See It

We struggle with responsibilities that are very important, but just can't figure out how to measure them. But we do know when we see them being fulfilled properly or when we see symptoms of a problem.

When this is the case, one technique is the *think in the negative* activity.

For example, a manager wants to address a core responsibility regarding teamwork with an employee. But the employee responds defensively with statements such as, "I'm a good team member. I show up for all the meetings. What else do you want me to do?"

This manager is struggling with identifying some behaviors or measures of good team performance. The solution is to think about it in the negative. What does "bad team performance" look like? When described in the negative, the question is usually answered with ease. Following are some examples of bad team performance observable behaviors:

- Not showing up on time – or not at all.
- Being physically present, but not contributing at meetings.
- Being negative – putting down everyone's ideas, but not offering positive suggestions.
- Not accepting responsibilities or assignments.
- Not accomplishing committed work on time.
- Playing to political agendas with other team members.

Reversing each of these statements to a positive expression of the same behavior provides a set of observable or measurable responses to this question.

Good team behaviors on the other hand include:

- Being present when requested or needed.
- Contributing at meetings – offering ideas and building on the ideas of others.
- Approaching problems with a positive orientation to find ways to solve the problems presented.

- Accepting and fulfilling team responsibilities and individual assignments.
- Meeting responsibilities to standard and schedule.
- Working with all team members to create collective success.

Here's another example of *working in the negative*. Writing good software code is an important goal, but not measurable as a simple statement. What is "good code" since software developers know that there is both subjectivity and art as well as science applied to writing software.

But if the question is asked, "What does bad code look like?" The answer might include the following:
- Does not deliver the functionality required.
- Delivers the functionality, but performance is poor - speed, responsiveness, etc.
- Lengthy, complex and redundant – more code than required to achieve specified functionality.
- Not robust – breaks with frequency – fragile.
- Number of bugs and complexity of bugs.
- Modularity and re-usability is very difficult.
- Hard to modify without major re-write or impact to other areas of the code.

When reviewed in the negative, it is easier to identify behaviors or measures of bad software code. Reversing the negatives to positives provides a number of factors that can be used to specify measurement criteria for software code.

When this technique is used to review responsibilities and goals, the measures become clear – resulting in a fully-aligned set of expectations.

Categories of Measurement

There are four types of measures – *Quantity, Quality, Time, and Budget or Cost.*

Quantity – How many or how much is accomplished? Typical examples include:
- Amount of sales revenue generated

- Amount of software code written
- Number of training programs conducted
- Number of customers contacted
- Number of units manufactured or produced

Quality – This defines the "how good" question. Quality may be based on objective data or subjective feedback. Subjective feedback is more useful if specific behaviors are identified as examples, or if inputs from multiple sources are used. Typical examples include:

- Performance level (operating speed) of software programs written.
- Numbers of bugs per 100 lines of code written.
- Percentage of orders requiring re-work for incomplete or incorrect information.
- Customer feedback/satisfaction from training programs provided.
- Team input and peer reviews.

Time – Most work is done to a schedule or performed within some agreed period of time. Time can be set as a specific date for the achievement of a task or goal or it can be a measure of how long a task requires to be accomplished – expressed as cycle time. Typical examples might be:

- Project to be completed by September 30.
- Report to be developed within the next 30 days.
- Fifty production pieces to be completed every hour.
- Percentage of airplanes that leave on time.

Note in the above measures that time may be its own goal – i.e. completion of a project by a certain date. But time may also be a symptom of other problems – very often quality problems. For example, airplanes not leaving on time are measured as a time issue. But a root cause analysis might show that the punctuality issue is due to a poor process in cleaning and turning a plane around – which is actually a quality issue. Regardless of the root cause the measurement indicator – time – serves as the basis for defining whether the performance requirement is being met.

Budget or Cost – The fourth measurement is cost. Typical examples include:

- Project to be completed with no more than 100 hours of work required.

- Units to be produced at a cost not to exceed $100 each.
- Cost of sales leads not to exceed $35 per lead.
- Cost of sales not to exceed 25% of total selling price.
- Training to be provided within the allocated training budget.

Every core responsibility can be measured using one or more of these four measurement criteria. There is no rule regarding how many measures to use, but recognize that measures will become the focal point for performance. Be careful not to measure what is easy to measure at the expense of what is important to measure.

For example, it might be easy to measure the number of sales prospects and the number of sales closes for a sales rep. However, if the goal is to improve sales performance, the critical measures might relate to the prospect qualification process and how the sales rep brings a prospect through the sales cycle. It is very important to think through the measures that are put in place and ask these questions: What are the likely intended behavioral consequences if employees are being driven to achieve these specific measures? What are the likely unintended consequences that will also be created? Are these the desired consequences? If not, do any measures need to be modified, or are other measures also required to provide a proper balance?

When managers and employees work together to create a fully aligned set of expectations, the output should include the following elements on one or two sheets of paper:
- The organizational vision, mission and core strategies.
- The purpose of the employee's job clearly showing its alignment to the organizational mission.
- A defined set (10-15) or responsibilities – each with a results focus.
- Goals under each responsibility where the responsibility needs further definition into specific goals.
- One or more measures under each goal or responsibility so that performance expectations are clearly understood by everyone.

This fulfills the 3 o'clock position on the performance management system – expectations are now set.

CHAPTER 10

Supporting Performance

Once the expectations have been set, the performance management process moves into the implementation phase – getting the work done. This is the 6 o'clock position on the performance management cycle and constitutes the bulk of the interaction between the manager and employee during the course of the year.

Managers have three tools at their disposal to help their employees be successful: feedback, coaching and counseling. Of the three, feedback is the most powerful.

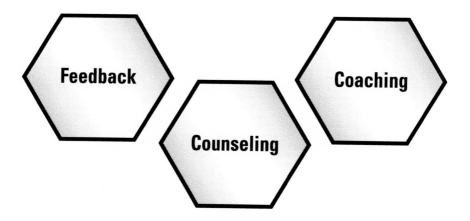

We all crave feedback. Everyone wants to know how they are doing. Even when people respond badly – with defensiveness, avoidance, denial, or even counter-attack, they are taking in the feedback. And even after the poor reaction, most people display some behavioral changes.

There are many excellent references and tools addressing coaching and counseling. In my own consulting experience I have discovered one tool that I believe represents the most powerful technique that managers can use to help their employees be successful. It integrates the concepts of feedback, reinforcement, inspection, coaching and counseling all rolled into one and can be one of the most mutually satisfying aspects of the relationship between managers and their employees. It's called the *one-on-one* and it is elegant in its simplicity. Here's how it works.

When your managers are asked whether they engage in conversation and feedback with their employees, the most frequent answer is: "Sure. All the time. We're always connected."

When the employees of these managers are asked the same question, they provide the opposite response. Their comments are more often like the following. "Are you kidding? He's always running. We talk in sound bites. We never have time for a real conversation about anything. And when we do talk about an issue, it's always about what needs to get done right then. We never have conversations about any longer term issues or about me."

The dilemma is that usually both the manager and the employee are correct. There is lots of conversation and interaction between most managers and their employees, but it is typically urgent and transactional. This leaves employees uncertain about other aspects of their work so they ask their managers for more information or input, which the managers reluctantly take the time to provide. Why reluctantly? Because they're busy, under pressure and want to move on to whatever's next on their own agenda. So managers want employees who work more independently. Employees want managers who will take the time to listen to them and help them with various aspects of the job.

The one-on-one concept is a simple and extremely powerful breakthrough to solve this dilemma. Very simply, it is a regularly scheduled meeting between the manager and his/her direct report. One-on-ones can be scheduled as often as weekly and as seldom as monthly. Meetings held less than once a month have difficulty maintaining communications continuity. Meetings held more than once a week border on micro-management and should only be used when detailed oversight due to performance issues are required. Most one-on-ones are scheduled for an hour and typically use 45 minutes to an hour in each session.

Here's how they work. The manager sets a pre-determined time with each employee for their one-on-one discussions. A regular specified day and time of the week should be established and treated with great respect by both parties.

The meeting should be divided into four segments. First, the employee should be able to ask any questions or bring up any issues or areas where help is needed regarding current work. The employee gets his/her questions answered first. Second, the manager goes over his/her list. That list might include checking up on assignments from the previous session. It might be a review of projects or it might be some new work assignments that the manager wants to give to the employee.

This part of the meeting should address the short term day-to-day business needs that keeps work moving along as required.

The next part of the one-on-one session provides an opportunity for the manager to select one or two other core responsibilities and guide a discussion around them. Some responsibilities will not need this separate attention – their urgency and visibility cause them to be addressed as an integral part of regular transactional business. Other responsibilities, however, may not be so visible. Longer-term projects, strategic initiatives, relationship building responsibilities, etc. may never surface in the course of day-to-day business. If the manager doesn't ask about them in these sessions, an entire year might go by without them being discussed. Then, when they are brought up at review time, it may be a surprise to the employee who forgot about them, or it may be a surprise to the manager to discover that areas he thought were being addressed were actually lying fallow.

Identifying one or two core responsibilities in each one-on-one that go beyond the issues of the moment keeps both manager and employee focused on the entire job.

The final part of the one-on-one session should be left open for whatever issues either party wants to bring to the table. This is a good moment for longer term goal setting or career discussions. It is also an opportunity to discuss broader organizational issues. The manager might use this time with the employee to solicit inputs regarding future plans. It is a place where the manager can empower the employee to contribute to the total business of the enterprise.

When managers are first introduced to the concept of one-on-ones with their employees as presented here, they often react something like this. "Are you crazy? That's a good idea, but I don't have the time. I'm already jammed with work and now you're asking me to add one hour a week – or every other week – for each of my direct reports. How am I supposed to find the time?"

That's a reasonable reaction from a transactionally challenged manager, but it does not recognize the reality of either the time or the benefit of the one-on-one model. When managers only work with employees in transactional sound bites, two huge time consumers are generated.. First, the manager is inundated with employee emails, phone calls, drop-ins, corridor conversations, etc. that often consume the bulk of the manager's time. Second, the manager is frequently engaged in re-directing work that was not being done the way he wanted. This consumes both his time and the wasted time of the employee who now has to re-do work because the directions and instructions initially received were inadequate due to the fact that the manager didn't have (or take) sufficient time to provide clear instruction.

In other words, there is never have enough time to do it right. But there is always have enough time to do it over. Ah well.......

The following example should illustrate my point. I have observed two senior managers in the same organization with relatively similar size groups and work of similar intensity and complexity. One manager is continuously harassed, overworked, and inundated with lines of people waiting to see him.

The other always seems to have time – time for employees, time for new initiatives, even time for his consultants (like me). The biggest difference I see is in the discipline of implementing regular one-on-one sessions. The transactionally challenged executive doesn't do any one-on-ones. Consequently, everything requires an urgent meeting and crises run the day. The other manager is personally planfull and relentlessly disciplined about his one-on-one meetings with his employees. His management team is competent and connected, and works autonomously between sessions.

Not surprisingly, the one-on-one meetings are also the ideal time for employee coaching and counseling. This model provides a level of communication in which managers and employees take the time to listen to each other and respect each other's thoughts.

As one of my personal mentors said to me many years ago, "The highest form of respect you can show someone is to take the time to truly listen to them."

CHAPTER 11

Providing Feedback

Of all the situations that arise regarding performance management, the question I am asked most frequently is, "Yes, but how do I deal with ……." This manager is now referring to his or her problem employee. The nature of the problem may vary. Sometimes it's a skill issue, although that is rarely the problem. Usually, it's about attitude. It's about the employee who has the skills and the potential but only does the minimum required, and the manager never gets much more unless she pushes for it. Or it's about the employee who is so negative and disruptive with fellow employees that he creates a difficult work environment for everyone. Or it's about the employee who makes a commitment, appears to work on it, but never delivers what was promised. The work product is always late, or incomplete, or has multiple errors, or wasn't checked. Or it's about the employee the manager really wants to fire, but doesn't know how because he wasn't clear about expectations and is concerned about being unfair, or even about the possibility of a lawsuit.

There are many variations on the theme, but the outcome is always the same. The manager is frustrated because he is somehow unable to deal with a difficult situation to either get the desired performance, or separate the employee from the organization.

Why is this so difficult? There are lots of reasons, but a few seem to stand out. See if any of these strike home.

- The manager isn't sure how to address the performance issue because he didn't really provide enough clarity about expectations in the first place.
- The manager finds it really hard to provide feedback because the problem seems to be a general attitude rather than specific issues.
- The manager is afraid that confronting the situation will only lead to an angry or defensive response, which may lead to even worse performance. So the manager decides that it's better to leave the situation alone and get whatever performance he can.
- The manager fears that the person will be so devastated or crushed that she will cry or be destroyed and then the manager won't know how to pick up the pieces.

- This person is in a protected class (age, sex, race, other minority group) and the manager fears that addressing the issue may lead to a lawsuit, threat of a lawsuit, or an accusation of discrimination.
- The manager is personally uncomfortable with confrontation and doesn't know how to approach the employee.
- The manager realizes that the outcome of the discussion may lead to the employee's termination. The employee really needs this job and the manager's genuine compassion prevents action, leaving the situation unchanged.

There are other reasons as well but these are a pretty powerful group of concerns that cause many managers to avoid addressing issues, even when they know they should be dealing with them.

The Consequence of Inaction

The dilemma is that lack of action rarely works. Very few problems or performance issues solve themselves over time. In fact, the opposite is more likely to be true. Lack of action actually reinforces existing undesired behaviors, with the effect that they tend to become increasingly severe over time.

Some managers wait until evaluation time and then blast the employee. This is equally useless and can actually be disastrous. Raising issues at evaluation or review sessions when no prior mention of them has been made is unfair to the employee. The reaction is likely to be quite bad and deservedly so. Performance issues should be addressed when they occur, not saved up in some little book to be unleashed like a nuclear bomb in the evaluation process.

Managers should identify issues when they arise and discuss them with employees right away. These feedback sessions can be quite brief and should have a problem-solving orientation. They should also be conducted in private. The most important aspect is to have the conversation rather than to ignore the behavior. Lack or action or overreaction doesn't improve the situation and is very likely to make it worse. Let's consider an alternative approach.

The Pygmalion Effect

The Pygmalion effect is the colloquial expression used to describe something more formally known as *expectancy theory*. Very simply, this means that the behavior of individuals is significantly influenced by what other people expect of them, and how those expectations are communicated.

The theory has been researched extensively, and proven time and time again. It really works. Let's look at the Pygmalion effect first from a positive perspective. How does a coach improve performance? By recognizing and reinforcing the good things that person does. By expressing his confidence in another person and then supporting and reinforcing good behaviors, that person develops confidence, which leads to improved performance.

Think about teaching a child how to ride a bicycle. The parent puts the child on the bike and tells her this is going to be easy. The parent holds the bike while their child struggles along and tells her what a great job she is doing. The parent tells her that by the end of the day she's going to be riding the bike all by herself. Then the parent begins to let go and every time the child rides a little bit without falling down, the parent praises her and tells her how good she is doing and encourages her to do more. When the child does fall down, she gets a hug and is put right back on the bike. The parent tells her that she knows she can do it and is there to help her. And it works. By the end of the day, the child is riding around alone and proud of herself for the accomplishment.

Expectations are communicated through behavior – sometimes verbal, sometimes nonverbal. Sometimes, behaviors are intentional and applied consciously, sometimes unconsciously. But the other person gets the message and responds accordingly.

Let's apply this theory in a work setting. You have two employees. Both were recently hired. For one, you have very high expectations. This employee went to your alma mater, impressed you in the interview, came to work well dressed, seems to be applying himself to the job and you think you made a great hire. The other employee went to what you considered to be a marginal school, but you needed someone so you went ahead and made the hire, although with some private reservations. Now the employee shows up and doesn't seem to be quite as quick at understanding what you want. So you say to yourself, "Uh, oh. I think I may have made a mistake."

Now let's look at what is most likely to happen. You are more likely to set higher goals for the first employee. You are more likely to recognize good performance in your preferred hire. You are more likely to give that employee more time and attention, helping him to get the job right. The consequence is that this employee blooms and does well.

What about the other employee? While you may not say anything negative, you don't give this employee as much of your time and attention. You don't set the standards as high. You don't recognize good results. You may not bother to correct errors – you've already started to write him off. This employee also "gets it" and the path to failure is set.

This theory has been researched in many settings and consistently validated. The classic example is the elementary school teacher who is given a list of her students for the new year. Half of the students have an asterisk by their name, indicating that they have been previously been identified as potential high achievers who are expected to bloom this year. But these students were selected at random – they are the same as the rest of the class. But by the end of the school year the potential bloomers have actually bloomed! They have higher scores on standardized achievement tests and also develop higher confidence and enhanced self-esteem.

The only difference was the expectation in the mind of the teacher. That expectation translated into the teacher's unconscious behavior and the students responded in kind. Expectancy theory works!

Why do we talk abut the Pygmalion effect in the middle of a section on feedback? Because it is quite possible that we, as managers, are unconsciously contributing to and reinforcing the very behaviors that bother us the most. Our expectation of how the employee is likely to behave and perform is transmitted unconsciously to that employee. So we need to check ourselves out and determine whether we are part of the problem, which may enable us to be part of the solution as well.

Personal Responsibility Applied to Feedback

There are two underlying principles that are requirements for a positive feedback session: personal responsibility and intentions.

Personal responsibility must be the foundation for employee feedback and performance improvement. It is also an integral part of the prior work in defining core responsibilities with employees.

Human beings are the only known sentient creatures on this planet. This means that people have the power of perception and the ability to make conscious decisions about their actions. How does this fundamental principle relate to performance?

The following diagram exemplifies the model. We are all impacted by stimuli – some internal, some external. Here's a simple example to demonstrate both types of stimuli. I have decided to lose some weight and I've chosen to go on a diet. I brought my lunch with me – a simple salad that I made last night. It's now 11:45 a.m. My internal stimulus tells me I'm hungry and a hamburger would be great right about now. That salad I made last night is not very appealing at this moment. In addition, my co-worker comes over and invites me to join her for lunch. We always have a good time together so I'm really tempted to go. That's my external stimulus.

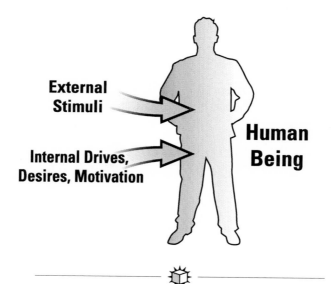

Now I have to decide what to do. Do I stay with my original goal which was to remain on my diet today or do I succumb to the internal and external stimuli that are encouraging me to do something else?

The result of my decision looks like this.

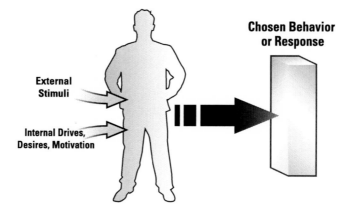

I choose my response…whatever it is. In every case, human behavior is the result of choice. The ability to choose a response to stimuli is the essential element that differentiates human beings from all other creatures. In between stimulus and response is a moment of choice. Sometimes, that moment can take days; at other times it seems instantaneous. But the response is a matter of choice…and therefore a matter of personal responsibility.

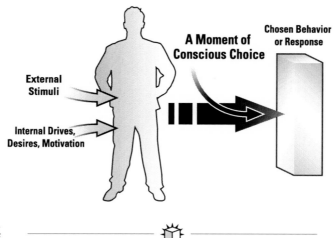

Let's examine this concept applied to a work setting. Imagine three colleagues who are working as a team on a project. They are going to meet with a manager whose cooperation is critical to their work. This manager has a reputation of being difficult to work with and they have been warned that he is not very interested in their project.

They go to meet with the manager and his reaction is predictable (perhaps some of their expectancy theory at work?). At any rate, he listens impatiently, disagrees with their assumptions, challenges their data, demeans their project, personally insults their intelligence, and challenges their intentions. They leave the meeting quite unsuccessful in their attempt to solicit his cooperation.

One of the three employees is quite angry and agitated. He says, "He had no right to talk to us that way. He really makes me mad."
The second employee says, "I wonder what we said that got him so upset. Perhaps there's another way we could have approached him."
The third employee says, "Well, I just consider the source. We'll have to figure out a way to work around him."

The first one then replies, "How can you say those things? He attacked our project and personally insulted us. He just makes me so mad!"

Now let's look at this scenario from the perspective of personal responsibility. These three employees shared similar goals and responsibility for this project. Their internal stimuli driving them toward success were similar. They were all in the meeting together and all heard the same response from this manager. Therefore, they were all exposed to the same external stimuli.

But their responses were all different. One of the three chose to become angry. The second chose to accept personal responsibility for the outcome. The third chose to remain emotionally disengaged and is seeking an alternative. These responses were all a matter of personal choice.

Based on their responses, each of these three employees might select a different course of action. The angry employee might choose counterattack or escalation. The second employee might choose to reframe the situation and go back to the manager with a new approach. The third employee might choose to change the project or find a different path forward.

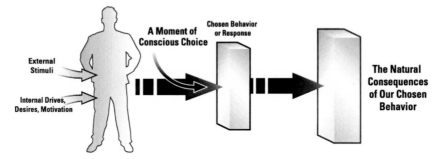

Each of those actions would lead to different results. The consequences of those actions would once again be the responsibility of those employees. The core principle here is that we are all responsible for our own behaviors and we are also responsible for the consequences of those behaviors.

When individuals choose their behavior, they also choose the consequences. "As we sow, so shall we reap." This fundamental concept is essential for a feedback session. It is the only appropriate response to statements such as:

- You're always picking on me.
- He made me do it.
- It's not my fault.
- They forced me to behave that way.
- If they would change, then I would change too.
- They make me so mad.
- Didn't you hear what the customer said to me first?
- Bad things always happen to me.

Feedback sessions are more successful when managers first establish the employee's personal responsibility for his behaviors, and for the consequences of those behaviors. Managers who conduct feedback by describing behaviors and their consequences are not *doing anything* to their employees. They are helping their employees understand the consequences of their own behavior.

If managers take the position of helping employees understand that they choose their own behaviors and the consequences are the natural outcomes of those behaviors, they can have successful and productive feedback sessions with employees. These sessions also tend to be quiet and rational, with minimal negative emotionality or flare-ups. This sense of personal responsibility is a fundamental building block of performance management.

Clarifying Intentions Applied To Feedback

The second major foundational element for useful feedback is clarity about intentions.

Why do managers give feedback? There are many possibilities. Here are a few of the most common reasons:
- To get it off their chest and feel better (also known as dumping).
- To bring the other person down a notch or two in size.
- To set the stage for future poor evaluations.
- To set the stage for future actions and documentation for future termination.
- To help the other person shift to more effective behaviors (the only appropriate reason).

Of all these, the last one is the only basis for a productive feedback session. All the others are self-serving behavior by the manager. Therefore, prior to having a feedback session it is important for managers to "check themselves out" regarding their own intentions. If they are really angry at that moment, they should not provide feedback. They should wait until they're calm and under emotional self-control. If managers are using this feedback discussion as the path to termination, then there is a specific course to follow which will be described later.

If the manager's intention is to help the other person be successful, he will use the positive aspects of expectancy theory. This is the basis for a good feedback conversation that can lead to genuine behavioral change.

Consider the following scenario. I had a sales rep who was really quite good. There were some areas where I thought I could help him improve his performance. But I noted that every time I attempted to have a feedback discussion with him, he became quite defensive. He would argue with me, disagree and justify his actions. I was quite frustrated as was he.

One day I said to him, "Mike, let me be clear about these discussions. I am trying to have a productive conversation with you. My goal is to help you be successful. It doesn't do me or the company any good if you're not as effective as you might be. So when I have these conversations with you, my intention is to give you the positive coaching that will help you achieve more success for yourself and for me as well."

He looked at me in surprise. He said, "I thought you were trying to beat me up. I thought all you wanted to do was to find fault with me. If what you want to do is coach me so I can do better, then I'm all for it."

We then had regular and quite successful feedback/coaching sessions.

Looking back, there was only one difference that occurred in our work together. The difference was in my clarification of my intentions and in his understanding and acceptance of those positive intentions. That made all the difference.

Conducting Feedback Sessions

If these principles are applied difficult feedback can be given in a very useful, effective and reasonably straightforward manner. Here are the basic rules for creating the right setting for a positive feedback session.
- Give feedback as soon after an event as possible. Our recall as human beings fades rapidly and the impact of history fades our memory as well.
- Feedback sessions do not require a lot of time, nor do they have to be a big deal. Most feedback sessions can be accomplished in about ten minutes.

- If either you or the other person are emotionally hijacked – angry, upset or embarrassed, then wait. Don't give feedback until both of you are calm.
- Find a private place. Don't conduct a feedback session in front of others – especially the employee's co-workers.

Once these conditions have been established, try the following steps for giving employee feedback.

- First, tell the employee that you want to provide her with some feedback about whatever issue you have selected.
- Second, state your intentions. "My intention in providing you with this feedback is to help you." Or, "I want you be more effective in working with this group and the purpose of discussing this with you is to help you do that." It may surprise you how much a statement of positive intention will remove defensiveness and allow the information you want to provide to be received.
- Third, describe what you observed. Do this as accurately and objectively as you can, without adding any judgmental comments. "I listened to your exchange with that customer. It got pretty heated, turned into an argument, and then she hung up on you." That describes what happened. "That was a rude and inappropriate way to handle a customer," is a judgmental statement and much more likely to elicit a defensive response.
- Fourth, ask the employee if what you just described is consistent with their view of what just happened. You might say, "Did I describe the situation accurately?" Or, "Would you like to add anything to my description of what happened?" There may be other information you are lacking. If not, the employee first 'agreeing to the facts' makes the next step much easier.
- Fifth, ask the employee what likely consequences will result based on their behavior. The consequences may be physical, behavioral or emotional. If the employee says "I don't know," or shrugs a shoulder, then press further. Ask them how they thought the other person felt. Ask them if they were the other person, what they would do next. This is not a new concept – we do it all the time when we are raising our children. Three-year-old Johnny

grabs a toy from three-year-old Sammy, and Sammy starts to cry. What does the parent do? The parent asks Johnny, "How do you think Sammy feels? Why do you think he's crying now?" This exchange is meant to build empathy and help young children understand the consequences of their actions. The same technique works equally well with adults.

Once you have worked through the likely consequences of the behavior, ask the employee to identify how he might have behaved differently. If the employee takes responsibility for his behavior and its consequences, and takes responsibility for identifying alternative behaviors, you are much likely to have that person implement those alternative behaviors in the future.

- Sixth, once you have decided on the alternative behavior, come to a simple agreement with the other person that that is how they will handle a similar situation in the future. This may be a defined statement, or it may simply be "I agree" or a nod of the head.
- Seventh, when you see a similar circumstance in the future, look for how the other person behaves. If they use their old behavior, it is time for another feedback session, a bit more forcefully or at least with a reminder of the previous discussion. If they use the new behavior, be sure to recognize it as soon as you can after the event. Continue to reinforce the new behavior until it becomes a habit. When new desired behaviors replace old undesired behaviors, you will have completed a successful feedback process.

Counseling

Sometimes, the feedback model doesn't work. Sometimes, managers see behavior that is so unacceptable that they feel they must take more aggressive action, especially if the health or safety of others are involved. Under these circumstances, they need the next step: a counseling session. Counseling sessions follow patterns very similar to feedback, except that the scope of the discussion is larger and the consequences are typically greater.

For example, suppose that you have been observing an employee who has demonstrated the lack of initiative in addressing customer issues on a repeated basis. You have encouraged and prodded him. You have given him feedback. You see a short-term difference after each conversation, but then the employee goes back to old habits. You are getting pretty close to the end of your tolerance level. It's time for a counseling session.

Before the session, be prepared. Pull together specific examples – even if these are the same ones you used in prior feedback sessions. Bring together any other data you have – including input or feedback from co-workers or customers. Then call the employee into a private place and let him know you need to have an extensive conversation together.

Once again, start with a statement of your intentions, even though the stakes may be higher. You might say something like, "We need to have a serious conversation about a topic we've talked about before: taking initiative. My goal in this discussion is to help you realize how serious a matter this has become so that you can examine your behavior and determine whether you are willing to choose to change it."

Note the choice built into that statement. Behavior is always a matter of choice. Human beings generally react badly when they think all their options have been taken away from them. This statement by the manager is a reminder that the employee chooses his behavior and has the right to continue to do so. But as the manager, you are now going to focus on the more significant consequences of those behaviors.

Next, ask the employee to identify the probable consequences. You might ask, "If you don't choose to change your behavior, what do you think the consequences will be?" Stay with this question until the employee is clear – either by his statement or yours – that in this case the consequences are likely to be severe – even the potential loss of employment if the situation warrants such action. Now the stage for performance improvement is set. As the manager, you have initiated the conversation, stated your intention, described the behavior and reinforced the consequences. The next step is to go to the heart of the session: corrective action.

There are two questions that need to be answered. The first is why the employee consistently demonstrates this behavior in spite of previous discussions and feedback sessions. Perhaps there is something about this person's situation that impacts their behavior. Perhaps it is such a deeply-rooted part of their character that they can't change it. Perhaps they don't care enough about their situation to be willing to change it. Or perhaps they don't have the skill to change it. Perhaps they lack the will power or emotional self-control to change. Perhaps it's something else entirely. But in this phase of the conversation, your goal as the manager is understanding. You want to understand why the person repeatedly demonstrates this consistent behavioral pattern.

Once you understand the underlying issues behind this behavioral pattern, you can select one of several possible alternatives. All alternatives start in the same place: reinforcing the consequences of this behavior. Based on the employee's answer to the 'why' question, you may follow several paths. The simplest is a re-statement of the required behavioral change with very specific, fairly short-term consequences if the pattern continues. In the most severe cases, this next part of the conversation may lead to the development of a mutual exit strategy for the person. In other cases, it may lead to skill development, coaching or other problem-solving strategies.

Regardless of the path forward, the final step of the counseling phase is to review the expected behaviors with great clarity about the consequences. Then be prepared to reinforce positive changes or immediately implement the consequences of the failure to change.

This may sound like a harsh process – also known as *tough love*. But it's certainly better than inflicting death by a thousand cuts. It's also the only potential way to change mutual expectations – the self-fulfilling prophecy – from a negative to a mutually positive path to success.

CHAPTER 12

Reviewing Performance

The final stage of the performance management process – nine o'clock on the performance management cycle – is the review phase. This phase includes performance reviews (evaluations), recognition, rewards, and linkages to compensation.

The Performance Review

How much planning and preparation is required for the performance review? If the manager has done everything else described thus far, the answer is "not much." He's already done it. If clear expectations and measurements were set in the beginning of the year and employees were empowered with broad responsibilities, they should have stayed on course and know exactly where they stand. If the manager conducted regular one-on-one sessions throughout the year he was giving and receiving feedback all along the way, and making course corrections as required. Therefore, there's not much left to do at the end of the year.

Year end reviews should begin like most one-on-one discussions, but with a summary of the entire year. The best technique is to ask the employee first to assess their own performance while the managers makes a similar independent assessment. Then both parties can compare notes, discuss and come to an agreement regarding any discrepancies (which should be very few).

This mutual review should be derived directly from the core responsibilities. Review each responsibility one at a time, against the agreed-upon measures. For each responsibility, determine together whether the expectations were met, were not met, or whether the results exceeded expectations. That discussion is far superior to any numerical value system.

If there are situations in which the employee did not meet expectations due to legitimate prevailing circumstances, that should be noted at this time as well.

At this point, the discussion should shift and look forward to next year. It's time to raise the performance bar – to move the employee along the performance scale previously discussed.

Start with a review of the core responsibilities. Are there any that are no longer appropriate? Are there some new ones that should be added? Then review the specific measures for each responsibility. Should any of these be changed? Finally, identify any specific goals under designated responsibilities where new challenges are appropriate.

Look for new opportunities for growth, or increased areas of responsibility. Stretch the employee's thinking toward higher conceptual levels, greater strategic inputs, continuous improvement, or development of self or others. All of these are areas where raising the performance bar can have significant meaning.

The remaining elements of the performance management process are recognition and linkages to rewards and compensation. Rewards are contractually agreed – not discretionary. Discretionary bonuses are not official rewards – they may or may not be provided by the organization or by the manager. But rewards such as commissions are a contractual part of an employee's compensation system.

Recognition

Recognition is described in its relationship to rewards, which is why it is in the nine o'clock section of the performance cycle. In reality, recognition should have been implemented all along the way. It should be practiced throughout the entire performance management process.

Recognition is discretionary and does not necessarily have any tangible product or financial value accompanying it. Telling someone their hair looks nice today is recognition. Showing appreciation for how a customer was treated is recognition. Thanking employees for a good job on a particular task is recognition.

All human beings crave recognition. Even those who say it doesn't matter to them crave it. Great performance strides have been made by giving people a coffee mug in recognition for a job well done, or acknowledging them at a meeting. Recognition is one of the most powerful tools for positive reinforcement that a manager has, and it's really easy to do.

Yet many managers seem to be reluctant to do it. Many years ago, I was consulting in one of the divisions of a very large defense company. This division had 8,000 engineers working on very complex innovative military technologies. I had the privilege of listening to a number of presentations being made by research teams to the general manager of the division and his core management team. The highest compliment I heard all day – by the general manager – was, "I don't see anything wrong with that." That was the highest praise given.

At the end of the meeting, I asked the GM if he ever considered actually telling someone they had done a good job or had a good idea. He said to me, "Oh, we don't do that around here. People should know they're doing a good job. If we have a problem with them, we let them know. So if they don't hear anything from management, they should just consider that they are doing a good job."

That didn't sound like a very inspiring work environment…and it wasn't. When you walked the halls and asked people how they were doing, the most common answer was, "surviving." Employee surveys showed the lack of motivation and every time the economy was doing well, this company's turnover exceeded the norm for its industry. People were bailing out whenever possible for more exciting work, even though their compensation and benefits were certainly competitive.

Recognition is simple. It takes ten to thirty seconds. Do it in sound bites, but be specific. "Thanks for doing a great job," doesn't have much effect because the employee doesn't know what they did that was great. "Thanks for handling that report so quickly," is much more likely to have that report prepared even more quickly next time.

Recognition should not be reserved for a performance review. It is good management behavior that should be implemented throughout the course of the year.

About Compensation

The prevailing thought among performance management experts about compensation is that it should NOT be directly linked to the performance management system and should NOT be an integral part of the annual performance review.

This runs counter to common practice in most organizations, so let's take a minute to understand the rationale for this perspective.

If an employee is going into an annual review and knows that the determination of his merit increase will be part of the discussion, then the focal point of the entire session (in the employee's mind) is negotiations. The employee will be very reluctant to agree to any performance shortfalls because the implication is that it might impact the merit increase. So the entire meeting is not really about performance, it's about salary. That's why performance reviews should be about performance – a review of the previous year with a primary focus on the upcoming year. If performance achievement levels are agreed, the compensation conversation can be conducted at a later date, and it will likely be very brief. The substantive part of the compensation discussion was already completed in the separate performance discussion.

Let's examine the myths and realities about compensation. Nearly all organizations have a salary-based compensation system. There may be some hourly employees, and some groups (such as sales) may have income based on commission. But most employees receive a base salary as their core compensation.

In most organizations, bonuses are not part of the baseline compensation system. Bonuses are based on company performance. Their distribution is typically discretionary, not contractual. Although bonuses may comprise a substantial part of an employee's income, they are not a core part of compensation. They may or may not be provided and the employee has little control over that fact. For this reason, salaries are the core of the compensation system.

Most companies say they have a merit-based compensation system. This may indeed be their intention, but it is typically far removed from reality in actual practice. The following example demonstrates just how constrained the compensation is in most organizations.

A company has salaries set within some number of ranges or classifications. Classifications may be many and narrow, or few and broad. But they are there – identified as the salary range for a position. That makes sense. A position only has so much value in the market regardless of the incumbent. If companies allow salaries for given positions to exceed market value, they place themselves in a non-competitive position. The best administrative assistant in the world, for example, has a value that caps at a certain level. If administrative assistants received salaries of $250,000 the company would be out of business. So salary ranges set the parameters of the potential salary for an employee in a specific position.

Most companies also have a policy regarding the scope of the increase allowed within a range – commonly somewhere around 15%. A 15% raise is a lot of money but it's almost never the reality that employees receive because of other constraining forces.

The company then establishes a percentage pool for salary increases – typically around 4 or 5%. This number was set by several factors. First, the financial performance of the company and its ability to provide salary increases is a primary determinant. Market conditions to remain competitive, which determine price limits for goods and services provided, are a second force. Current rates of inflation and cost of living are a third force. How well the company is competitively positioned to attract and retain talent is a fourth factor. After all relevant factors are assessed, some overall number is determined. This percentage of current salary levels becomes the pool of eligible funds for salary increases.

The next challenge is the distribution of this pool among employees. If the company has 1000 employees, that overall percentage works fine...theoretically. The highest performing employees can receive 15% increases while others receive nothing based on performance issues, keeping the overall total to the limit of the designated 4 or 5% of current salaries.

The dilemma is that this 4 or 5% number is translated down through all levels of the organization until the first level manager receives the same requirement – provide whatever salary increases you want within policy (0-15%), as long as you stay in the range for each employee's position. But don't exceed the mandated 5% average. That creates a real dilemma, because this first level manager is likely to have 5-8 employees. If this manager wants to give a superstar a 15% raise, then the other employees will have to receive very little because the average can't exceed 5% and there are only a handful of employees in the pool.

So the reality facing this manager is a range of 4-6%, not 0-15%. There might be exceptions, but only if he is willing to "rob Peter to pay Paul."

This situation is compounded further by many other factors that affect how much of a raise will be allocated to an individual. Consider the following additional factors, which are just a few of the many considerations:
- A person's salary compared to his/her peers.
- The relative position of salary in its range – the more an employee approaches the top of the range, the less the raise is likely to be.
- Inequities that need to be resolved – either under or overcompensation.
- Changes in the market value of a position.
- Education and credentials.
- How easy or difficult it would be to replace this person.
- How much noise the person has made.

When all these other complicating factors are added to the equation, there is depressingly little left over for actual performance-based or merit-based differentials. This is why the best exercise in compensation often remains an attempt at damage control.

Pay-For-Performance Compensation Alternative

The only way an organization can truly address performance-based compensation differentials is if it has a system in which salary is baseline compensation, and a true pay for performance system is allocated for virtually all positions. In such a system, salary is determined by the market value of the position, factoring in such modifiers as education and experience. But it is not a merit-based or performance-based determination. All individuals in the same position with comparable education and experience receive the same base compensation.

Then a separate performance-based pool of funds is set aside for actual merit considerations. The size of the pool is guaranteed, its allocation is not. Thus, individual annual differentials can be given to reflect true performance outcomes. These performance-based increments are not permanent or cumulative. They must be re-earned each year.

There are some aspects of an organization in which this system has been in place for years. Sales is the most common example. It is not unusual to find a sales force in which every sales rep receives the same, or very similar base pay. This base pay represents a small percentage of total anticipated income. The rest of their income is based on their commissions, which have to be re-earned every year. This is a true performance-based system.

The most common arguments that are made against performance-based programs for all employees are as follow.

*Argument – **That may work for sales because it's so measurable. But a lot of what people do is not as measurable so it would be hard to implement.***
> *Answer:* Traditional goal-setting systems do indeed have this problem. If the system described in this book is used, then responsibilities are clearly defined with measures for each responsibility. Defining the measurable difference between meeting expectations or exceeding expectations (achieving stretch goals) is built into this model. That can be the basis for allocating performance-based compensation differentials.

Argument – A lot of the work that people do is dependent on the output of others. So individuals could be hurt by this system through no fault of their own.

> *Answer:* That's true. But it's also true in sales. A sales rep may be hurt because the company produces poor products, or because customer service is below par. An individual sales rep may be hurt because his biggest customer goes bankrupt and he had nothing to do with it. The reality is that virtually everyone works in an environment in which many factors outside of their control can influence their success. Every job includes the challenge of creating success in spite of external factors.

Argument – There's no extra money. How do we fund the performance pool to get a system like this started?

> *Answer:* Start by taking your planned merit salary pool for next year. Let's say it is 4%. Use 2% for general increases to account for inflation and cost of living. Set aside the other 2% to begin the performance-based compensation system. Then, as employees leave the company through natural turnover, look at the salary used for their replacements. If the new hire is starting at a lower base salary (often the case), take the differential and add it to the performance-based pool. That might bring the pool up to 3% of total salaries. Next year, when the company would have allocated 4% for its merit salary pool, do the same thing and the performance pool will now be up to 5%. Over the course of a few years a very substantial performance-based resource pool can be created.

A Personal Example

The following story is true, developed from my own consulting practice.

A number of years ago, I had a fine group of very talented and able consultants. The consultants had five primary responsibilities:

- Provide direct consulting service to their clients.
- Manage client accounts and consulting projects.
- Sell consulting services to new and existing clients.

- Contribute to the company's development of new products.
- Contribute to the overall leadership and administration of the company.

I used a typical salary-based compensation system, with discretionary bonuses based on company and individual performance. Salaries were all in the six figure category, with a differential of about 20% between the lowest and highest paid consultants.

My frustration was that all the consultants did a fine job of serving clients (the baseline performance standard), but beyond that there were wide ranges in performance. Some were good at project and client management, others were not. Some were good in sales, others were not. Some contributed to new product development; others did not. Since delivering service to clients was the core competence and represented their primary role, I didn't want to force movement in the other areas for fear it would negatively impact their primary responsibility. The biggest shortfall area was sales.

As a consequence, my company was stuck. I personally sold 50% of the company's business and all my consultants collectively sold the other 50%. I didn't want to hire a separate sales force. The only path seemed to be to grow the number of consultants, but that was a linear growth path. I wanted more.

So I changed the compensation system dramatically. At the start of the new year each consultant received a new salary base – approximately 40% of their previous salary. Every consultant received exactly the same base – no differentials at all. Then I added performance-based compensation as follows:

- For every dollar that a consultant delivered, he/she received 20% of that revenue when it was billed.
- For every dollar that a consultant sold, he/she received 10% of the revenue when it was billed, regardless of who did the work.
- For every dollar a consultant project-managed, he/she received 5% of the revenue when it was billed, regardless of who sold it or who delivered the service.

- Contribution to new product development, leadership and administration were assessed through a 360° feedback tool in which every employee in the company participated.

The consultants initially reacted with dismay. They all complained that they would make less money and they all threatened to quit. So I built a transition plan in which I guaranteed them the same income they made the previous year for the first two quarters, while also calculating and showing them what their income would have been based on the new system. The new system actually took over in the beginning of the third quarter.

What were the consequences? Several things happened.
- Every single one of them made at least what they had earned before – all but one made significantly more.
- The size of the company doubled over the next three years, based on the additional sales generated by these consultants.
- The previous income differential between consultants had been 20%. The differential was now in excess of 150% - with all of them having the same base pay.
- Different consultants were skilled in different areas – some only wanted to deliver services, some enjoyed sales. Since the system allowed each consultant to emphasize their preferred areas – understanding the consequences of their behavior, there was a self-leveling feature.
- Every year, we conducted a team feedback session based on the 360° process. This was used to allocate compensation for contributions for both product development and leadership, plus any additional funds in a bonus pool based on company performance. Through this frank and open discussion, individual consultants periodically "fired themselves" when they recognized that their own performance did not meet the standards of their peers.

The overall consequence of this system raised the performance bar at both the individual and the company levels from good to great. The company grew, clients were more satisfied, consultants enjoyed their work because they focused on what they did well, and they made higher incomes as well. It was a driving force for a significant change – not because of the compensation alone, but because the compensation system was now fully aligned with the performance management system.

Linking Performance Management and Compensation

Based on these concepts, it is easy to see that discussions about performance and compensation need not – should not – be conducted at the same time. One will unduly influence the other if they are linked in the same conversation.

Let's assume that your organization is retaining a merit-based, salary-driven compensation system, and is also implementing a performance management system similar to the one described here. Under these circumstances, consider the following possibility for implementation.

The performance review should be about performance. A mutual assessment is completed and the core responsibilities and measures serve as the agenda for that review. The focal point of the discussion starts with a review of the previous year, but rapidly shifts to the upcoming year, and the performance expectations for next year are set.

Now, quite separately in another meeting and at another time, the employee receives salary and merit increase information. Because merit budget increases based on salary are so tightly restricted by so many factors, there is minimal value in attempting to tie them explicitly to the performance discussion. Certainly those who exceed expectations should receive a greater increase than those who did not. But the merit increase differentials are unlikely to match the actual performance differentials. The performance difference must be addressed through discretionary bonuses, recognition, career advancement, and the personal satisfaction that comes with high achievement.

In a merit-based salary system, performance management should be about performance. Compensation should be loosely linked to performance in that higher performance should yield higher compensation over time. At the same time, suggesting that a particular rating in a performance evaluation will yield a particular percentage in a salary structure will so politicize and contrive the system that it can create quite a lot of damage.

A Final Word

This book is intended to help managers understand the critical value that performance management can have for individuals and for organizations. Among all the tools available to companies, there is nothing that comes close in its ability to energize human performance and create a competitive, sustainable advantage for an organization.

I hope that the readers of this book take this to heart and use this tool for the betterment of themselves, their employees and their organizations.

Bibliography

Bain & Company. "The Ultimate Question." Ongoing research. See www.bain.com, 2007.

Buckingham, Marcus and Curt Coffman. *First, Break All The Rules.* New York: Simon & Schuster, 1999.

Corporate Leadership Council. *The Hard Truth About the Soft Stuff.* Summary of Performance Management Strategy Research. Washington, D.C.: Corporate Leadership Council, 2003.

Covey, Stephen R. *The Eighth Habit.* New York: Free Press, 2004.

The eBay Company. www.ebay.com

The Gallup Organization. *"The Employee Side of the HumanSigma Equation."* The Q12 research and programs. www.gallupconsulting.com. Updated annually, 2007.

Harris Interactive.com. Research updated annually.

Joyce, William, Nitin Nohria and Bruce Roberson. *What Really Works.* New York: HarperCollins Publishers, Inc., 2003

Reichheld, Fred. *The Ultimate Question.* Boston: Harvard Business School Press, 2006.

Resnick, Harold S. *Leading for High Individual Performance.* Module Four of the Work Systems Associates, Inc. Leadership Development Program. Ponte Vedra Beach, FL: Work Systems Associates, Inc., 2006

Resnick, Harold S. *The Impact of Human Performance on the Bottom Line.* Presentation made to Financial Executives International. 2003.

Resnick, Harold S. *Reinventing Your Organization to Achieve Sustainable Breakthrough Results.* Work Systems Associates, Inc., 2002.

Schein, Edgar H. *Organizational Culture and Leadership.* San Francisco: Jossey-Bass Publishers, 1985.

Harold S. Resnick

 Dr. Harold S. Resnick is recognized internationally as a leading authority in organizational transformation, performance management and leadership development. He has consulted with hundreds of private and public sector clients in North and South America, Europe and the Middle East.

In 1980 Dr. Resnick founded Work Systems Associates, Inc. (WSA), a management and organizational development consulting firm. He served as its CEO until 1998. Under his leadership, WSA grew to become a multi-national firm serving such clients as CH2MHILL, EMC, Novell, IKON, Raytheon, ABB Lummus, Volvo GM Heavy Truck, Philips Electronics USA, Lockheed Martin, and Shell Oil.

In 1996 Dr. Resnick founded Generation21 Learning Systems, one of the seminal web-based training and knowledge management platforms. It was the technology of choice by NASA, Dell Computer, Agilent Technologies, and Verizon. Generation21 was acquired by Renaissance Learning, Inc. (Nasdaq RLRN) in July, 1999.

Dr. Resnick received Master's and Doctoral degrees from Wayne State University. He was a university professor at Boston University, Temple University and Wayne State University. As a corporate executive he was the Director of Organizational Development for Raytheon Data Systems, supporting 5,000 individuals in 147 locations around the world.

Dr. Resnick and his wife Barbara reside in Ponte Vedra Beach, Florida where he maintains a private consulting practice serving clients in performance management, organizational change, leadership development, strategic planning, and executive team development. Previously published articles are archived on his website, www.worksystems.com.